Weather
Without
Technology

David King

GREEN MAGIC

Green Magic
5 Stathe Cottages
Stathe
Somerset
TA7 0JL
England
www.greenmagicpublishing.com

Designed and typeset by K.DESIGN
Winscombe, Somerset

ISBN 9780995547827

GREEN MAGIC

Contents

'Day unto day uttereth speech and night into night showeth knowledge'

(PSALMS 19 VV 2).

Introduction

Predicting advance weather at least one growing season (90 days) ahead without recourse to using any technology, but by using nature, flora, fauna, animals, birds, nature, the moon, tried tested and reliable saws/sayings, local data and experience.

If our forefathers, without recourse to any technology, managed quite successfully to advance predict the seasons, and survive, then why cannot we do so now?

Therefore over some 40 years I have researched, collated, defined and now use a methodology resultant from all that experience to forward predict, by at least three months, what the collated data tells me, and publish this quite openly for all to see and enjoy on my website.

This book therefore is a book of the website content with greater explanations that the reader can pick up and delve into.

The object being to educate, entertain, interest and introduce the reader to this different method of weather predicting, to teach how to look and actually see what nature, animals, birds, plants and trees are actually telling us about what is present and also, more importantly what is to come, from such observation. Therefore the aim is, by the end of this book, to hope that every reader will have a better knowledge of how the weather affects and is affected by nature and much to do with nature, and increase their knowledge of just how magnificent nature is.

The Professional side of Weather Recording

I was for over 20 years an active participant in the Royal Meteorology Society but left after a divergence of thoughts and methodology, I still retain an interest however.

I am an active member of COL (Climatologist Observers Link) and submit daily data to the Met Office Weather Observation Website and BBC Weather schemes.

I have a fully functional Met Office standard weather station in the back garden in a Stephenson screen containing certified maximum, minimum and standard thermometers, wet and dry thermometers, hydrometers, Mb pressure gauges plus two Tinytag recorders which I download once a week to the computer database here.

Additionally I have a Davis VP2 radio weather system complete with UV and solar instruments, that again automatically download to the computer here at 10 minute intervals. I have two R&D Electronic sunshine recorders on the roof of the house, plus two separate anemometers for wind measurements.

A further German made automatic weather station supplements all the above, plus range gauges across the garden in addition to the Davis system.

I therefore have a fully functional independent weather station that accurately records all weather data here. Such records go back to 1985 and are continuous.

Additionally I keep a contemporaneous daily record every four hours from 0800hrs to 2200hrs of actual visual recording and observations.

Therefore I have a reasonable working knowledge and functionally accurate daily record of actual weather. Such records and data is incorporated into the methodology used here.

So, despite using a completely different approach to weather predicting I can combine both systems for even better results.

Not a complete Luddite then!

The Author

I am a self-taught amateur climatologist with no scientific training or qualification of any description. I was for many years an active Associate Fellow of the Royal Meteorological Society, and am currently a member of Climatologists Observers Link (COL). I regularly appear on TV and radio and my articles appear in national newspapers and magazines in addition to local BBC Radio and local newspapers and magazines. I have a free open website, www. weatherwithouttechnology.co.uk. I was born in Yelverton, Devon where my interest in natural history was stimulated within the broader family, who later moved to London.

In 1957 I started as a uniform beat policeman working the Clapham and Nine Elms part of south London, for those unfamiliar with this area, it is the area south of the river Thames

bounded to the west by Chelsea Bridge and to the east by
Vauxhall Bridge and inland to Clapham Common, then along
the main road eastwards to the Oval by the Cricket ground and
tube station, there it turned north and ran in a straight line to
Vauxhall Bridge. It was an area with green common at Clapham
and Vauxhall Park, but mainly working class residential area
of Edwardian buildings and 1960's style high rise flats. There
was much light industry and, as you got nearer to the river at
Vauxhall a huge industrial complex of the Old Covent Garden
Market, on the side the river Thames with main loading and
unloading bays for the coal, refuse and other barges. The other
side of Nine Elms Lane consisted of the main freight depot
for Southern railways catering for all the fruit and vegetables
for the adjacent market; the Stewarts Lane engine sheds (all
steam and smoke), Carlsberg and Meux's brewery, a large
coke plant and several engineering plants plus also, in season,
French Onion sellers from Brittany. The police station itself
was an old Victorian building directly opposite what was at
that time Battersea Dogs Home, the road leading up to Chelsea
Bridge had Battersea park to the west – and remnants of the
Festival of Britain Pleasure park from 1951, and to the east
Battersea Power station, gas works, gas holder and parts of the
rail freight yards – all beneath one of the largest railway inter-
sections at the time since all trains to Victoria and Waterloo
stations passed through this Nine Elms sector.

It must not be forgotten that in the late 1950's London
Docks were still the largest docks in the world bar none, and
although big ships travelled no further than London Bridge,
much of the cargo was transhipped to barges and travelled
west along the Thames. Primary cargo was coal for Battersea
power station and adjacent gas works, plus too, coke for the

massive gas and coke works also in Nine Elms Lane. It was therefore a really busy place twenty four hours a day.

I was warned by the older coppers never to walk down Nine Elms Lane on the river side, since the rats that lived on the coal and other barges were bigger than cats – and if hungry would eat you......ha ha. Until one night I disregarded this advice and as I walked along the riverside wall (five foot high) the biggest rat I have still ever to see, jumped from a barge onto my back and knocked me over – I kid you not. So I never walked riverside again. If, whatever the time or day, you walked from the police station at Nine Elms to Vauxhall along Nine Elms Lane, you would emerge at Vauxhall covered in coal dust from the coke works, smuts from the engine sheds and grime from the general environment, you were quite dirty indeed, and also it was the 'fag-end' period of the great London smogs so you also came back dirty yellow colour, those were the days!

To see that area now is a revelation, embassies, smart million pound residences, high rise apartments and a clean river. No coke works, no gas holders, no engine sheds, a brand new Battersea Dogs and Cats home and no police station.

The river Thames at that time was a cess pool of everything imaginable, you name it, it went into the river, dead animals, human bodies, flotsam, jetsam, wood, anything and everything you could think of, plus too the unseen killer of germs in the river. If you happened to get immersed in Thames water and took a mouthful, then it was a three day stay in St Thomas's hospital to make sure you were OK. Needless to say, you stayed out of the water. However, the sole exception to this was if there was a human corpse or body on the foreshore – a pretty regular occurrence too.

If a Thames Police riverboat was handy and could get to it the they would slip it into a body bag and take it away. If however, it was out of their reach and was accessible from the shore then it was finders keepers. Why so? Wages in those days were not great the Edmund-Davis pay rise was still years away – as were white shirts too. If you recovered a dead body from the foreshore there was a £5 bounty – nearly a weeks wages – it gets better – if you then searched the body, another £5 – and if you fingerprinted the body, yet another £5 – so riches beyond compare. Being fortunate to have been trained in taking fingerprints I therefore was often asked to do the search and fingerprints. What a bonus – despite a gruesome and dirty job – just goes to show you, some people will do anything for money.

However from this majestic river I learnt about tides, river flows, currents, the effect of the moon: I can also remember in the early 1960's when I was a 'Noddy Bike' rider, (remember those, the Velocette 250cc air cooled twin grey coloured motorcycles so beloved by the riders) riding my motor cycle from Vauxhall Bridge along Albert Embankment towards Lambeth Bridge, on the pavement in two feet of flowing dirty Thames water as the Thames overflowed with flood water. The road was too deep for the bike and as such impassable. We now have the Thames barrier – but it was a frightening sight – the water kept coming over the wall. I think of this water when I see all these magnificent high rise buildings on the Thames the sea side of the Thames barrier and just wonder if sufficient thought has been given to rising water levels. So life at Nine Elms was interesting to say the least.

I learnt the effect of the spring tides, ebb tides, high and low water, currents all from just leaning on the bridges and watching plus some in depth reading. I soon became adept at tide times too. At the same time I also learnt about clouds, weather signs, when to, and not to, take rainwear, when to and not to take unnecessary outer clothing, how to keep cool when all around is sweating bucket loads, how to conserve energy, how to keep warm in bitter weather in those days, vital, since you walked on your own with no contact at all with other officers. The winter of 1962/3 a classic – when all the buses and trains still ran despite the snow and ice. I was taught astro-navigation by ex World War Two RAF bomber crew copper and qualified in that skill too. The makings of a future hobby were firmly established.

In 1964 I then went to outer London, Croydon – a city in itself, very gentrified, very green and so different from Nine Elms. From there I moved to real countryside at Kenley (famous for the WWII RAF Kenley fighter station). A different world. An example, on night duty, there was a sergeant and three panda cars plus one man inside the station, so five at best. At 10pm on Sunday nights a full roast dinner was prepared and the man inside was charged with cooking it ready for us all to sit down at 2am for roast dinner. After the meal back out to work again. Who covered the ground – an agreement with Croydon (the parent station) gave us cover – sometimes the Croydon inspector for the night ate too – would that be tolerated now – forget it. Sadly the station at Kenley – another Victorian building has gone – never to be replaced. At Kenley I did a stint as 'infection control officer' manning a disinfecting station at the entrance to Cane Hill Mental Hospital at Coulsdon where during the foot and mouth outbreak they had to first isolate and then destroy all the farm animals at the site. So less 30 minutes from central

London I was a real 'country copper.' Some adventure then.

Here I learnt about weather elements, the sky at dawn and night, what birds and animals did, when they migrated, when they nested. What time of the year butterflies appeared and disappeared, flowers, trees and plants all came under the microscope. How fogs formed, how cold it was before ice formed or melted, how snow drifted. All good solid basic information and the future was now set. So now I had to get real saws/sayings about weather lore and such matters from real country folk and a new chapter in my life fully opened, after I left the police force in 1984.

Collecting the Data

In the early 1960's around the peripheries of London were numerous cattle markets, and as such, wonderful places in which to find the eponymous older sage, he with the hat and walking stick and bags of common sense and full of knowl-edge and understanding, a veritable walking encyclopaedia of folk lore and weather data.

It was to these markets and others in Kent, Surrey and East Sussex that visits were made. Being a street-wise working copper, talking to and respecting people was an everyday natural event, retention of conversation too was an acquired skill, therefore on such a visit the above eponymous sage was sought out and the introduction went something like this 'excuse me boss, I am doing research for a book on country sayings and weather lore. If I buy you a pint to start with, will you please be able to give me an hour of your time and knowledge on such matters, without any rubbish or bull-shit, which I will write down here, and, at the end of the hour I will buy you another pint together with a pie or wad as a thank you?'

I was never refused, and over a 10 year period I recorded some 800 such conversations – all written in longhand into A4 sized books; a true treasure trove of knowledge – and it also cost a bomb in beer and food, but priceless.

The next stop were the records/archives at Canterbury and Rochester cathedrals and Westminster Abbey (St Peter's), here at the first two I found a 'moon lore chart, that dates from about 1150 AD that is basis even now of my methodology. The archives at the Bodleian library, the National Archives, the House of Lords and Commons Libraries; all local county record offices; all local parochial church records, newspaper archives, old book shops and libraries were all searched and researched, all yielding snippets of information. So at the end of research in the early 1980's I had reams of hand-written data in A4 sized books, newspaper cuttings and other such paper work, plus too in the course of collecting much natural history information too.

The problem now was how to put all this into some sort of form?

Computers were just starting and I took at course in BASIC language, at least a start, albeit laborious, but a start. Fortunately Bill Gates heard my prayers and cries and in-vented Windows 3–1 just for me, halleluiah!

I sat down and started to transpose 10 years of research and data into some sort of system, and started a spreadsheet, database and word system; which after two years began to give some form to the subject.

I reduced some 50,000 saws/sayings to less than 10,000, which in the passage of time is now some 5,000 but all if used skilfully and in the correct context, are reliable, trustworthy and proven, and now form part of the current methodology.

It took another two years to produce an intelligent practical spreadsheet and data sheet for each month of the year. Therefore now, each monthly entry to the website contains; a preamble – a place where I can inform, educate or comment upon current issues or topics; a datasheet – that contains all the monthly events in date order plus too all the relevant saw/sayings for the month; an easy reference spreadsheet – enabling the reader at a glance to see each day in précis form; finally the compilation of learned research of respected meteorologists concerning each month.

To enable such data to appear on each spreadsheet some 40 different items of data are included; it is akin to a massive jigsaw, where each piece on its own mean little, but when fitted into the plan provides a perfect picture.

In the 1970's when I started to do serious research there was no internet, therefore all research had to be done 'on the hoof,' actually physically travelling by whatever means to the sources, wherever or whatever they were and painstakingly looking for clues. At the start I was to say the least naive, I knew roughly what I wanted, but not exactly, so I grabbed everything there was regardless of usability – if it looked helpful then it was collected. It all was written in long-hand too.

The face to face interviews commenced in the late 1960's and were, to say the least, pretty raw, but after the first hundred or so a pattern evolved and developed, I then had an agenda to ask or prompt, without interrupting the flow of the interviewee, but could add as supplementary questions. In hindsight I wish I had gone back to see some of the original interviewees, but over 10 years some die, some move on and of course after foot and mouth most cattle markets ceased to exist, but one learns with experience. I learned to establish exactly the area where the interviewee lived and worked, any speciality he had, what he liked, disliked, abhorred or dreaded, and why. Were there any local places that would help the research, where were the local records, anything that would improve the knowledge? To use knowledge gained from my previous occupation – to get a full picture of as much as I could, and then use it to the best of my ability.

Now in addition to interviewees, local church records, local newspaper records, local town hall records going back in some cases hundreds of years became accessible, and an open book – therefore the next move had to be Cathedral archives.

Cathedral archives are priceless, for they are accurate, written by experts and contain such wealth of information of former times – in itself a problem, for in many cases no indices exist, but also a lot is written in French-Latin from the days of William the Conqueror, plus too the word symbols/ letters too in many cases are different.

I therefore started in the year 1100 AD at Canterbury Cathedral. To get there I had to make appointments and request the reason – but, as with other such places of knowledge and learning, being humble, but inquisitive and showing interest with a desired aim, soon gained the respect and assistance of the archivists, especially with difficult translations, but all for a good cause. It took about a year to do the records at Canterbury Cathedral, many long hours, page by page, year by year and I ceased about 1450 AD since I had the crux of what I needed.

The next port of call was Rochester Cathedral with an identical method, agenda and time span to 1450 AD. A lot of what I found at Canterbury was duplicated, but from different sources, therefore corroborating both sets of data, which was both pleasing and informative; so that now much of the current methodology dates from 1100 AD incorporating facts from this research. The primary aspect being the moon lore charts explained later in the book. Despite their being from near 1000 years ago they are still so accurate that I use them all the time; over some 30 years I have made some slight changes but nothing to alter the basics – yet I am told by 'experts and scientists' that all I have is 'mumbo-jumbo dear boy, no scientific data to prove your point;' (how condescending from educated persons, who rely on computers from the early 1980's to base their assumptions on!). Maybe now you see why I parted company after some 20 years from the Royal Meteorological Society – it is their loss, not mine.

To widen the search I then used the archives at Westminster Abbey (St Peter's) and again the magnificent help and assistance from the archivists there was invaluable; and whilst there I did the basis of research into here where I live, Edenbridge, concerning climate change and farming husbandry from 1150 to 1731 AD. Research here was some six months, but I combined this with the House of Lords and House of Commons Libraries, just across the road since there too was copious history and data.

I now had a very good picture of what I wanted, so the single interviews continued unabated, but also enquiries were made of the Bodleian Library at Oxford, the magnificent history library at Exeter University, and their wonderful teaching and research staff.

The National Archives at Kew also welcomed me many times, especially since I needed the language skills of their archivists with many French-Latin documents, but never was I refused access or assistance, always a pleasurable and knowledgeable experience.

County record offices too, Kent, Surrey and both East and West Sussex added to the knowledge, all priceless. All local/regional newspaper archives were trawled too, some real pearls found here, but interestingly some stories from interviewees proven, and in few sad cases also debunked, such is life, but also shows the value of checking, proving and verifying; therefore when I now state that the eventual 5,000 saw/sayings I currently use are reliable, verified and proven I can say this with 100% certainty.

As the research continued and broadened I realised that other cultures too had much to offer, therefore a lot of time was spent in research libraries on the Druids and other pagan sects, for all have something to offer. The North American Indian culture also manifests itself in so many ways, especially concerning the moons and seasons, all such cultures have their uses and all have mentions throughout this book.

I made visits to the Met Office library and archives at Exeter and benefited from the data there, again the archivists and assistants always helpful and obliging. I am so honoured to have been helped by so many such informed and educated persons.

The final source was old book shops, such a magnificent source of tales, stories, saws and sayings, how sad that these treasures are now dying out. If I had to start my original research project now from nothing, all I would have would be the internet, plus the archives; but not the undoubted skills, knowledge, enthusiasm, pleasure and recollections of bygone years from so many interviewees. I feel so honoured to have been able to collect such memories from so many people, places and resources. I hope by this book, that I can pass on some of this knowledge to each and every reader; please garner and retain this knowledge for I fear you will not find so much knowledge contained elsewhere than in this one book. Sadly, although we are losing such old skills, I hope this book will engender renewed interest.

Yes, I know the data in this book is mocked, belittled and ridiculed by some, such is life, you cannot please all the people all of the time – but, if the book pleases some of the people some of the time, then job partly done; I say partly, because the aim is to try, the target is always 90% minimum, to be able to give a 90% correct prediction at least one whole growing season (90 days) or in some cases two growing seasons (180 days ahead). Sometimes it is 100%, sadly sometimes it goes wrong, that is invariably because somewhere I have missed, wrongly calculated or misinterpreted a vital fact, that has skewed the methodology. I always correct and apologise if that occurs, but for the greater part, the methodology is good.

I never claim to be perfect but the satisfaction of foretelling weather at least 90 days ahead and when the time arrives being near spot on is indeed satisfying. 'I told you so,' does not go amiss either!

So you can see that in actual fact it took over 12 years. The book is as good as the data I can put in it, I have endeavoured to do the impossible – to be able to give you advance weather to as high degree of accuracy just using what is out there – there is no technology involved, everything is explained in simple terms. Our forefathers managed to do it, and survived – that is my target. Please enjoy the read, it took a lot of time and effort to put together, but the result is well worth it.

So who were these interviewees?

I am asked 'who were these people you interviewed.'

The quick answer is anyone who lives in a rural community and works and has contact with the land and that community – which tells you absolutely everything and nothing.

So let me expand starting with the cattle market, nowadays a remnant of past glories, long lamented too, for many reasons such rural meeting places are becoming rarer and rarer, which is really very sad, for they are the life blood of the community, the weekly or fortnightly meeting place where gossip was exchanged, friendships forged, money made and money lost.

My first tentative visits to a market was locally at Sevenoaks in Kent, not a massive event as such, but a weekly meeting place for the rural community, with cattle, sheep, pigs amongst the larger animals but also chickens, ducks, geese, rabbits even the cat, dog or ferret too in the pens and cages. Add to this flower sellers, plant sellers, nurserymen, seed merchants, farmers sundries men, locally produced food products, the baker and you now get the general feeling, plus the tea stands, fry-up places, and, in season, either sarsaparilla or ice-cream salesman. A friendly place welcoming and inviting yet selective and private at times, but always the centre of news, gossip, rumour and 'have you heard' or 'did you hear,' or 'fancy that – whoever would have thought that!'

So into this world I stepped, and looked and watched, observed, made notes and assessed my chances of learning something. My first 'victim' was an old farm labourer – about 70 years old, weathered lined face of many summers and winters, a wiry frame, precious little fat, but muscular and fit, with hands both large as a bunch of bananas but hard as leather yet smooth too, he sat on a boundary wall, old flat cap on head, gnarled well worn walking stick in hand, wearing the inevitable countryside corduroy trousers with footwear of heavy leather boots. I sidled up to him said good morning and asked him if he could help me.

He looked me up and down and asked 'how?' I explained I was doing a weather project from old sayings and I wished to get as much first-hand information as I could, preferably from those, like him, who knew – without any bull-shit. He smiled and said 'you reckon?' I said 'yes' and explained that in exchange for a pint he could chat to me for an hour I would make notes – after the hour, another pint and a pie or wad. He thought about for a while and said 'OK' but no pint to start with, he pulled an old battered pipe from his pocket, looked at it, looked at me and said 'it needs St Bruno rough cut!' so I said OK and went to make off to the nearest shop to which he said 'where be going?' I said 'shop for backy,' he said 'nay go over to brown van and tell Pete, Harry wants usual,' indicating a battered old brown Ford van that had seen better years – to describe it would be DSAR = dents and scratches all round, perfect description. I trundled off to the van and Pete watched me coming, more in apprehension I thought, but he asked what I wanted and I told him. He looked me up and down and sideways – as all tobacco barons do – then said 'you straight?' I replied 'as a corkscrew,' and he opened the back and from a cover of dirty old sacks revealed a tobacconist shop of considerable quality and quantity, taking from it a tin of St Bruno – and as he did so, said 'you ain't seen nothing – got it?' I said 'don't know what you talking about,' paid him my dues and walked back to Harry; I was aware of all eyes watching me intently as I did the walk. Back with Harry he told me to sit down as he filled his pipe then lit it with a couple of matches and blew the smoke into the air, watching it rise to nothing….'OK my boy' he said, 'where do we start?' He chatted for an hour, he started from school at 14 on the farm with all the dirty jobs, he graduated to a herdsman over time, ploughed the fields with horses, did not fight in WWII as he was reserved occupation – but had bad feet – that on a farm too, made me smile. He was a wiley old sod, as sharp as a tack, missed nothing, asked where I was a copper and I told him London, but we got on famously we had a grudging respect for each other, but I was sure we could do more together, we got up crossed the yard and into the pub where I bought him a pint and a pie.

Being a stranger I got funny looks, but a copper gets used to this, so no sweat, when asked who I was, he openly told the assembly I was a copper from London – and few took quick gulps at that – and I was researching old saw and sayings, and that I would welcome more such chats. There was a general murmuring and nodding and shaking of heads, and the spokesman stood up and said OK, 'we'll help ee each week, but no snitching, cos you'll hear and see things that you don't see – get me?' I said 'trust me one day you may need my help,' and with that more drinks. I was now at least welcomed, so a good start.

I then chatted with a few, took some names and addresses, thanked everyone and had a wander around the market that was beginning to wrap up. The auctioneer came across and spoke to me and in a roundabout way asked my business, so I told him and seizing the opportunity asked him for a chat too, this took him back a bit, but he recovered quickly and said I was to go over to his shed in twenty minutes. I wandered around and in the due time knocked on his shed door 'enter' was the reply and I found some 10 persons all sat there. Question time for sure, but all went well and I was invited back next week, but also given a list of names and occupations plus a few addresses – all wanted to help. I thanked them all and left and made my way back home – a successful day for sure. The only small feeling was 'would they trust me?' Time would tell.

That evening I edited the first chat, and the circumstances, examined the list they gave me and found a complete list of trades, occupations and 'odd-jobs' (those that go from place to place doing 'odd-jobs.' Simple really) and drew up a sort of agenda for the next visit there.

The biggest local market was Maidstone, the County Town that had everything, cattle, fruit, vegetables, seeds, sundries, a full market everything you expect in a rural county town, so, at the end of the week Maidstone it was. This a different ball game, I knew no-one, no friendly faces, time to absorb the atmosphere, use eyes and ears, just take it easy and trust your luck. Two hours later I was still trusting the luck and lo and behold the auctioneer hailed me 'what be doing yere then?' 'Same as Sevenoaks' I replied 'but I know no bugger, so is hard work' – no problem he said 'tag along behind me and watch, I'll help ee.' So I tagged along for an hour as he auctioned the cattle – an education for sure – but fascinating. He did the last pen and passed his books and stick (auction stick) to his assistant and put his arm around my neck and half dragged me, in a friendly way to the local pub, where immediately on entry a pint was set up for him – and he said 'one for my boy here,' and said 'cheers my son,' as we drank up. I went to buy him a pint and he said 'you my guest I pay.' Well yes, I was his guest and he paid – well sort of – two more pints came across the counter, no money changed hands, so I said nothing.

Now, this really was not so strange, I was a copper in London, you lived, worked and survived with the help and consent of the people, you treated people as you yourself would wish to be treated, with kindness, civility, kindness and courteously – unless the situation called for a different strategy, live and let live was good motto. So as a working copper in a working class part of London, you were tolerated, and up to a point, respected – if you earned it, but also part of the community. The law was there, it was black and white at each end, but in between it was all shades of grey – and these grey bits were your working zone, use you head, think ahead, don't be foolish, be fair and considerate all come into equation. Get it wrong and you are in deep shit – get it right and you are everyone's friend – so experience is everything. A saying comes to mind 'knowledge is knowing that a tomato is a fruit, understanding is knowing that you cannot put it in a fruit salad.' If you master this, then you are halfway home.

So looking after the local copper is the norm, and, in return when problems arise you are expected to be fair, honest and do your duty. Hence the free beer for the auctioneer – he is the same to the rural fraternity – look after him and he will look after you. It was called 'The ways and means Act.' It worked. Impossible now of course, since everyone is perfect!

So the auctioneer took me aside and for an hour gave me more detail, a friendship was struck – that lasted 25 years until he died and I paid my farewells at his graveside. He too gave me a list of people to talk to, where to go and what to see – the ball was now rolling.

The friendly auctioneer was a wonderful stroke of luck, as from the word go, we hit it off, and, as is often the case in rural areas he was also a land agent/estate agent, he too wore big boots, but brown ones and brown corduroy trousers and invariably an Harris tweed jacket, with brown leather arm-patches; sometimes too a deer-stalker hat, always in his hand a clip board, sometimes too he smoked a cheroot, but he knew everyone, the good, the bad and the ugly. Over time, he counselled caution, suggested I see so and so, or visit this place or that, I never once saw him put his hand in his pocket in a pub – such is life, but he was shown respect, earned respect, and gave respect, bit like a street copper really.

I continued at Sevenoaks market as the main source for interviews, it was nearer, had a large friendly catchment area and slowly I got accepted into the fraternity of the market, slowly the suspicion of a copper from London wore off – and trust evolved – a two way street, kind of 'you scratch my back and I'll scratch yours,' but as long as the information I sought was rolling in, then no problems. I kept up the interviews, some better than others, some not so good, but you take the rough with the smooth. The beer bill slowly rose too.

I spoke to a labourer who still ploughed with horses and told me how the different weather condition made the difference to the ground, when to plough and when not to plough, how deep to set the traces and why. I spoke to the farrier, who knew everyone too, I learnt about different shoes, and why and also when not to shoe, why you should never shoe in some conditions – all grist to the mill, but all with a little more information, the data kept coming in.

Interviewing Sources

As a change from the market interviews, I decided to have a look at a few old local church parochial records and see what I could find, which would entail finding a suitable guide, and then trying to get into the records themselves, however, not with pint of beer bribe approach, maybe something different, like humbleness and guile – true an unusual combination – but if you do not try then you do not get; In for a penny, in for a pound.

When I was still at school I was a choir-boy at the local church, twice on Sundays and Sunday school in the afternoon; however weddings and funerals were extras, therefore I had good grounding in Christian values and fellowship, and with a father who was Chief Petty Officer, RN, you toed the line – dead straight line too. My father imbued with a quote from Hamlet too; 'Neither a borrower or lender be; for loan oft loses both itself and friend, and borrowing dulls the edge of husbandry. This above all; to thine own self be true, and it must follow as the night the day, thou canst not be false to any man.'

So with such advice and Christian virtues I hit the world. I was no innocent, in younger days the buyer of beer in bottles paid a deposit – returnable on the empty bottle – so they were hunted down, a penny on some but two pence on others. The empty siphon of soda water was the real prize, five shillings – a king's ransom indeed, it was no wonder therefore that, with look outs in place, one climbed the outside wall into off-licence yard, and having found the siphons, 'recycled' them over the wall to the boys outside. It was then out of the yard, wait a bit, then nonchalantly amble into the off-licence and claim the kings ransom on the empty siphons. Share and share alike was the watchword – and if caught, no snitching either, else you got drummed out of the gang. So with such wealth it was then into the grocery store and buy a bag of broken biscuits three pence a bag, so no more hunger for a bit. From there to the fish and chip shop and ask for the batter scrapings in a bag – all free, therefore street wise was the watchword – even for a choir-boy.

The Christian church has a strange hierarchy for those who serve the clergy, there was the vicar, in charge, he might have a curate to assist, he might even have a lady-worker to help with welfare matters; but he also had Vicar's warden – a local do-gooder – maybe the fore-runner of neighbourhood watch co-ordinator – nose everywhere – we've all met them. My dad was vicar's warden. He sat in the front row on the right facing the chancel, on the corner seat, so everyone knew he was there – it was his seat. There was also a People's warden, he stood up for the rest of the congregation, he too sat in the front row corner seat, but on the left. These two effectively ran the church – they had a committee called the Parochial Church Council – from whence all directives flowed – who in turn deferred to the vicar.

Back to church records; with such a hierarchy the best approach had to be from the ground up, and where better than grave-digger/sexton, for he knew everything that went on, sometimes too, on high days and holidays he would go to church. I sought out an old church with a lot of history and a most informative churchyard of headstones – such monuments tell you so much about the community, who was rich, the big families, the not so well off, the poor, all life is there – even in death there is segregation, but we are all equal, just that some are more equal than other.

I found my grave digger, why is it that most grave diggers are old, of small stature, hardly bigger than the shovel they dig with, and thin too? They seem to revel in working in shirt sleeves, even in the depth of winter; but they are strong, truly strong with physical strength that belies their stature. I feel sure that if they fell into a completed grave they would never get out as they would never grip the top! I told him who I was, what I was researching and if possible if he had any country lore/sayings I would welcome them, but I would like to see the oldest church records. He leaned back on his spade, gave it some thought, leant over and reached into his jacket on the next gravestone, from which he produced his pipe and backy plus a box of matches. 'Make yourself comfy and I tell e' he said, I leaned against a headstone a he slowly filled his pipe, tapped it, then put it to his mouth and lit it, puffing like a small tank engine pulling out of a station until it was smoking well. We chatted for an hour or so and he said he had to stop as he had to finish the grave today but that if I came back tomorrow at 10am he would take me down to the records room. I helped him as best I could in my amateurish way to finish the grave and pile the dirt to the side. He had a chuckle at that and told me that in another five years I might make a half-decent grave digger, but not before. I walked with him to the gate where he bade me farewell and rode off into the distance on his rickety old bicycle. I left and first stop was the tobacconist where I bought him some tobacco and matches and pipe cleaners ready for tomorrow.

Tomorrow arrived and I met as arranged, and gave him the gifts, for which he thanked me profusely, and went to the church. He unlocked a small side-door and we entered and I followed him into the church then down some stairs, through another locked door and into a quite large room that must have run under a quarter of the church at least – lined with shelves of books, files and papers. He told me sit at the small table whilst he went and sought some reading material for me, coming back with really old volumes from the early 1700's. Despite his apparent lowly position as a grave-digger, he was intelligent, very knowledgeable too, and he could read old English script better than I could a standard book. He impressed me with his skills and knowledge, though his hands were hard from digging, he had seen better times. However he led me through the volumes showing what people died of in the past, how much they paid for the funeral, how some were paupers and the church paid the fee. He kept up too, a constant barrage of old saws/sayings, and who in the village now he would trust (very few) and those he would not (several).

I sat there and worked out that at one time he was very clever and held a position, but, that something drastic had happened, and that position had been taken from him – a kind of sixth sense.

Reader let me digress for a moment please. As a copper in London I gradually learnt from the best university of all, the University of Life, where you see all, you learn so much and most of all you develop the skill, the essential skill of, within at a maximum of ten seconds, most times less, of arriving at a scene of an event and making an assessment of the situation. The longer you do it the easier it gets, cock up to start with and all is lost – so you learn by trial and error to know – that sixth sense. I had this sixth sense now, so I tried my luck on him.

I thanked him for his valued assistance to me and asked if he could direct me to another good source to increase my knowledge and understanding, to which he agreed, then he turned to me and told me I was quite shrewd too, since I had come to him and no-one else in the church, but he liked that. So, taking the bull by the horns I asked him who grassed him up, what for, and what did he go to prison for? He took out his pipe, slowly and deliberately he filled it, put it in his mouth, and then lit it – just like that tank engine again. He sat back in the chair and puffed into the ceiling – he looked at me and he said you a good copper my son, what you think I did? That put me on a spot; I told him that I thought somewhere along the line something had gone wrong and as a result you ended up in the nick and lost everything … He said nothing for quite a while, he tapped his pipe on the side, looked at me and said, 'yep – I had an affair with a girl in the village, but she was married – her husband came after me with a shot-gun – they was scuffle, the gun went off and he got shot.' I let him go on and said nothing. He then told me that the man would have bled to death had he not stopped the bleeding, that people heard the shot and came out to see, including his wife. 'The outcome was I went to the assizes and was found guilty of GBH and got 15 years. I was a single chap then but was an accountant; I lost everything and never recovered.' He divorced his wife and left the region much later.

I came out of nick with bugger all and started afresh – but no-one would employ a jail bird – so I had to scrounge around and find what I could. I ended up a few years ago dig-ging graves and here I is. I both empathised and sympathised with him, I thanked him for telling me and he thanked me for listening. He told me he would always talk to me, his knowl-edge was indeed deep. We tidied up the room, put the books away and went up the stairs into the church, then through the door out into the churchyard again.

He asked me how far I had come with the research, and I showed him what I had on me but said it was coming along. He asked me how many women I had spoken to and I told him none, which surprised him a bit, he said nothing but sometimes body movements speak louder than words. 'If you would like to talk to a really interesting woman I can give e one' he said. I said 'yes please – if it ain't a problem.' He stopped walking looked at me and told me to open my book 'write this address and name down my son, he said. 'go see her and tell her what you told me about your research – she will be a mine of information for you – yes really, you will get on well with her for sure,' I wrote the name and address down it was a couple of hamlets away – long cycle ride, but alright in a car. 'She's got a phone too, he said, and gave me the number. I wrote it down. 'A friend of yours?' I asked, he said 'kind of – I loved her then and I love her now to this day – go see her, don't mention me please, but when you've seen her come and tell me friend!' 'Shit' I thought,' he wants me to see his long lost love.' So I told him yes, thanked him for his help, shook his hand and watched him ride off down the road on his rickety bike – I hadn't a clue of his address either. So, a challenge is a challenge, and next job is to make a meet with his love – ain't life cruel at times.

The Diversity of Interview Sources

Whilst the markets continued to provide such a cornucopia of information and informants, some trades/professions/occupations never get anywhere near such markets, apart from the odd visit; the skilled vocation of coppicing and hedge laying is hardly seen, sometimes it appears in demonstration form at country craft shows, the sight of this interwoven ash and other hedgerows is now a dying art and skill – sometimes, very rarely though such a skilled worker will appear in order to see if he can obtain replacement tools, like a hook or saw. I had the good fortune to interview two such skilled workers, both well into their sixties, both rotund, physically strong but with such delicate skills when man-handling an old hedge into a brand new coppiced hedge – such a well laid hedge will last for many years and improve with age, with the absolute minimal care too. These workers had infinite knowledge of different woods and plants, what birds nested where and when, their knowledge of useful saws/sayings seemed inexhaustible, they were more than happy, provided I did not hinder them in their work, to chat as they worked, how sad such a normal countryside skill from the past is now dying; and interestingly too they drank tea at work and worked near a whole full day without break. Both in due course I took to the local pub and imbibed with them, and, at the same time opening the door to more such old skills and saws and sayings.

Another such worker was a really a carpenter cum woodworker cum a bit of everything. He owned two cross-bred shire horses and to these he attached traps or slides. A slide is a large hand built box not dissimilar to a toboggan, but bigger, the two I saw were some eight feet long, maybe a shade longer some three feet wide, a sold base but with curved skids/slides on the base exterior, and the sides about three feet or so high and the front and back sides were detachable. In narrow lanes in nearly any weather condition the slide would be coupled to the horses with tackle and harness, the horses would then drag this slide along through lanes, fields anywhere off the metal surfaced roads, where vehicles could not get, the loads and type of loads this transported was near endless – except pure liquids, liquids were carried in milk churns, which fitted well into the slides. Such men too had a wealth of weather lore, countryside knowledge of everything in the countryside too. I found over eight years just two such men, both sadly in their twilight years, both complained that no younger person was willing to follow in their steps, but of course now the quad bike goes some way to solving the problem, but it not as serene or peaceful or as calming as the horse and handler of the past.

Another group never seen at the market are the paid members of the hunt, true the hunt is followed by most in the true countryside, therefore most market persons are familiar with it. I will not go into the debate about fox-hunting, except to say that if you are not a true born and bred rural person, then with respect, you have no real qualification to have it banned. I was introduced by a farmer to the kennel man of the local hunt – a paid employee of the hunt, whose job it was to raise, care for and look after the pack of dogs of the hunt, he was the one who 'fosters' the younger dogs for a while to other hunt followers as they grow up, sort of puppy walking. It was his responsibility to train the pack to hunt. Feeding such a pack is a costly business, as are vet fees and other such necessary expenses; it is therefore no wonder that at times, and I appreciate times they are changing, rapidly – and did so after foot and mouth and after the 'hunting with dogs' legislation came into force, but there are times when the phone call from a farmer to the kennel keeper will solve two problems concerning some dead animals, ridding the farmer of the carcase and feeding the dogs. Excuse some of the wording, for over time, some of the correct phraseology has slipped me by, but bear with me please. The kennel man had assistants both at the kennels and on the hunt, and one of their names was a 'whipper-in,' who at times encouraged the dogs to act to commands and not go off and be 'free agents,' as was their wont at times, these men also were the kennel keepers too. Their knowledge of flora, fauna, animals, birds and general countryside matters was indeed vast, we had a few most interesting 'pow-wows' around the kennels table, or sometimes in the local pub, but all contributed to my knowledge and data collection. They told how the moons affected the hunt, the why's and wherefores, and the 'never to,' rules they adhered too. Some of their saws/sayings alas I found not be up to the standard of others, and over time, were discarded, but those that remained were pure gold dust and are dotted across each month of the year – even those months after Easter when the hunt does not operate. So thank you kennel men for your wisdom and entertainment, well worth every minute of time spent with you.

Every now and then I would get an invite from an inter-viewee at whatever market I was at, having spoken to him, to accompany him back to his abode for a meal and meet the family, most times I accepted, there was the odd, thank you but no thank you, time, but for the greater part I accepted – it would have been seen as bad manners to have declined, and having spent so long building trust, stupid to refuse. Once you get a black mark in such communities it stays! It was therefore not uncommon without any prior notice from her husband, that he would appear at the door of the kitchen with a stranger, me, and introduce me to the Woman of the House, his wife. They were always un- abashed, 'excuse the mess, but if I not know you acomin afore then accept this is my house.' Who controlled the house then? ha ha . It was always the kitchen – the living room was 'Sunday, high Days and Special days only,' my grandparents had the same rule too – and it was always best clothes in the best living room too – and no eating there either – invariably the door was locked to keep it clean and sacrosanct too; it as the only room in the house where the very best bone china was served – or seen too. One of the features of a farmhouse kitchen is the Aga cooker/range – comes with the territory – invariably positioned on a large flagstone floor, and equally with a clothes horse suspended above it, and the permanent heated kettle at the end. Most times too there were plates in the warming oven. A large solid wood table surrounded by chairs on three sides is the centre point – three sides, since the wife needs access from the table to the Aga for a multitude of reasons – that is all her workspace – enter it at your peril. Over the years I enjoyed many such visits and when the husband went to do other things then these women would chat away to me quite happily, their knowledge too was magical – they had, considering many rarely left the farm, infinite knowledge of all the goings on in the community too, but then the postman and other such delivery men spread the gossip/news, time really had no place in such a community, if it got done OK, but there is always tomorrow. I learnt much from these women, many of whom were expert vegetable gardeners too, who used the full moon phases for planting; and on this subject I learnt enough to write a book too such was the detail I absorbed.However it was not always one way traffic, many a time I got asked about 'so and so who lives down the side of the hill,' or who did you see at market last week, or who sold what, or how long was someone in the pub for? Caution always had to be the watchword, one word out of place could start an eruption for sure, therefore I always thought carefully on every reply I gave, and before replying asked myself why – I had so many confidences by now that I had to be careful, extra careful.

So over the years, I saw people come and go, times changed, the ravages of swine fever, bird flu, foot and mouth, stupid health and safety legislation, the hunting ban all played their part in a rapidly changing landscape, and how politicians used the rural community as a 'punch bag,' no, not harsh comment either, a truthful comment. I spent some twelve years speaking, enquiring, visiting such people and communities, twelve brilliant years; true hard work at times but honest work, well, maybe as straight as a corkscrew at times, but honest and true none of us is perfect. The knowledge I learnt, gleaned and collected concerning weather is all in this book. I doubt you will find a more comprehensive collection anywhere, if you get as much enjoyment from the reading, as I got from the research, then you too will be satisfied.

To all those I interviewed, became friends with, and many still remain so, the archivists, the research assistants, the linguists and interpreters, the librarians, keepers of records, book shop owners and all those that have helped me in the past, a massive thank you, without you all this would be impossible, if by any chance I have missed you out, please forgive me, there are so many you and has taken so long, the memory does fade. A couple of stories here you may recognise, but no names to embarrass, no fingers to point either. You all did me well. I hope in this book I return your trust and understanding

What is Omitted or Excluded from the Data?

I do not use any modern technology; the aim is to create a prediction using just what was available to our fore-fathers – the only exception being Met Office stormy and quiet periods and Buchan warm and cooler periods, plus perigee and apogee.

So modern meteorological language and theory is not included, which is not to say that some or all of the following were not in existence when our forefathers did their predictions, it is that I can find no instances at all of any mention of anything below in my research; and the simple reason for that is that such things were not yet discovered.

The following therefore, whilst everyday language for weather forecasters, presenters and journalists, plus those in the meteorological world, do not feature in any way shape or form in my predictions; they just do not exist in my methodology. OK, so I may penalise myself and therefore, without this modern knowledge, not be able to produce such accurate predictions, but I am not a Luddite and therefore accept these omissions as part of the restrictions on the methodology; but regardless, the predictions, even with this lack of data, are extremely accurate.

This list is not exhaustive but the main exclusions are as follows: Jet streams; blocking patterns; La Lina; El Nino; North Atlantic Oscillation and stratospheric connection; Pacific oscillation; Atlantic sub-polar currents; Gulf stream; Volcano effects; Greenhouse gases; Ozone layer; Solar variability climate change; Global warning and finally the Lorentz Chaos theory.

I hear the question why? A few years ago I did another project to discover why the part of Edenbridge where I live is named Spitals cross. After much research (running parallel to this weather research at times) I found the answer, but also some most interesting weather detail emerged too; and everyone now talks of global warming, the causes and effects etc; but this climate change is nothing new.

I commenced research into Spitals cross in the medieval period 1100 AD when the original name of Edenbridge first appears, and found that at that time there was a Mediterranean climate in this region; grapes, maize and other such central European crops were grown; but also the this climate and the influence of the Crusades meant that Leprosy was rife too. A Spital was a leper hospital, normally outside the main town, downwind, and was an isolation unit comprising of some six or so buildings with its own fresh running water source (nearly all the places in the UK with the word Spital in the title were such leper hospitals, eg Spitalfields in London, the Spitals interchange in Lincolnshire, and also all of interest, on the main Roman routes) and also on the main roman road joining Lewes in Sussex to Deptford in south London.

In the early 1300's the climate changed and in one year in the 1340's there were nine months of frost here in Edenbridge. Move to the 1580's and the Reformation and the climate was again hot with drought a common feature. Into the 1740's and it was so cold again that all the rivers froze solid (as did the river Thames).

So what is there so different about the current variation in climate? A personal theory is that it may well be cyclical; therefore, as shown above, it may well be that start of a climate change period, but that does not interfere with my predictions.

Learning the Data and How to Use it

The researched material collated into some sort of order revealed that most of the original data dating from as far as 1150 AD is based upon the Christian calendar. In medieval times the most educated person in the locality was the priest and as such was the fount of all knowledge. The centre of each locality was the church, whose bell was rung to signal the start of the work and again to end the working day. Every one went to church, everyone knew the Holy Days, the Saints days and other important days; equally everyone knew the phases of the moon, the rising and the setting of the sun; the start of the four seasons therefore it was logical use such Holy and Saints days as markers for the calendar.

Therefore the annual calendar is based on Holy days, Saints days and other important days, a recurring theme.

Some such Holy/Saints days are fixed, Christmas Day is fixed; some however are movable and depend on the moon to determine the date, Easter being the classic example, and from this date, everything before this date, Shrove Tuesday onwards, through Easter to Corpus Christi is dependant on the position of the moons to fix Easter.

The attached list of such dates for 2016 is as follow:

Holy days, special days and significant dates 2016.

Candlemass	2nd February
Shrove Tuesday	9th February
Ash Wednesday	10th February
Palm Sunday	20th March
Maundy Thursday	24th March
Good Friday	25th March
Easter Sunday	27th March
Low Sunday	3rd April
Pastor Sunday	10th April
Ascension Day	5th May
Chestnut Sunday	8th May
Pentecost (Whitsun)	15th May
Trinity Sunday	22nd May
Corpus Christi	26th May
Michaelmass	29th September
All Saints day	1st November
Advent Sunday	27th November
Christmas Day	25th December

There are some whilst not Holy/Saints days, that also are movable, such as Chestnut Sunday – always the second Sunday in May.

The next chapter will define the Christian Saints/Holy days relative to the Days of Prediction.

Days of Prediction

There are 13 days of prediction, 12 are fixed dates and one, Good Friday, is a movable date, and these occur each month except in October. They are a fair indication of weather and happenings up to the next such day, but, they are not to be taken in isolation, since this might tend to give a false impression, it is therefore imperative that they be used in conjunction with all the other tools in the methodology.

All the notes concerning days of prediction are taken directly from Uncle Offa's book, natural weather wisdom.

The author has annotated any comment where necessary, and this is so noted.

Days of prediction in detail:

25th January
St Paul's Day, also known as St Annanias Day

'If St Paul's Day be fair and clear
We shall have a happy year.
But if we have but wind and rain
* *Dear will be the price of grain.*
If clouds and mist do mark the sky
Great store of birds and beasts will die.'

Another from Devon:

'If St Paul's Day be fine expect a good harvest
* *If it wet or showery be expect a famine.*
If it is wind expect a war.'

St Paul is said to reveal the weather for the year ahead. This is a good guide for the first six months, but after that tails off somewhat. However, it has been known to be 90% correct and in one year, 100% correct.

Authors Note – *Having religiously followed the following instructions by Uncle Offa for 15 years, the best result was 80%, and I found that up to the last week of June it is quite reliable, alas, after that it does tail off rapidly.*

When following the weather on this day, it is necessary to observe and note down its phases hour by hour, or even every half hour throughout the day from 6am until 6pm. This is due to the belief that the hours of the day will reflect the weather month by month throughout that year. Generally such signs are dependable to the end of July, but diminish thereafter.

2nd February
Candlemass Day

At this coldest time of the year, this day has a host of sayings.

'If Candlemass Day be clear and bright
Winter will have another flight.
But if it be dark with clouds and rain
Winter has gone and will not come again.'

'Cold weather at Candlemass means colder weather
after the feast than before.'

'If Candlemass be bright and clear
Half the winter is to come this year.
If Candlemass be stormy cloudy and black
It bears winter away on its back.'
From Wiltshire.

'If sun be bright on Candlemass Day there will be
more frost after the feast than before.'
From Nottinghamshire.

'Where-ever the wind is on Candlemass day
There it will stay to the end of May.'

Authors Note – *this is near 100% true and so reliable too.*

Candlemass is the first of the Wind forecast days that are worth noting for they tend to be very reliable.

However, this wind day is not a true 90 day period (see Quarter Days), being out of sequence it is therefore to be treated with some caution.

21st March
St Benedict's Day – also a Quarter Day

'As the wind is on St Benedict's day.
So it will stay for three months.'

[very true]

This is a bold and emphatic statement that sometimes may sometimes appear to contradict St Paul's forecast. However, St Paul's day states the weather in general and makes no comment about wind direction.

Following St Benedict the next Wind day is St John on 24th June (Mid-summer's day), being just 96 days later.

Be guided on the wind on this day, and if the wind at Candlemass and St Benedict are contradictory, then St Benedict takes precedence.

Good Friday – Palm Sunday

Good Friday is Christian Day and a moveable feast, and as such deserves some explanation. For this purpose one has to include, for historical reasons, Palm Sunday too.

It is asked how Neolithic forbears managed to make predictions about Palm Sunday and Good Friday, especially since both are movable Christian feasts.

The answer is the name Easter, which derives from Eastre, the Saxon moon-goddess, whose festival was celebrated about this time of year.

Following the Lunar year, March 21st the equinox was then New Year's Day and the festival was celebrated at the first full moon thereafter.

When the early church was being established, it took over the festival for its own celebration, and so Easter came into being as the first weekend after that full moon.

The Day of Prediction may have been the full moon in past times, but today it is regarded as Good Friday.

> *'If on Palm Sunday there be rain, that betokened to goodness.*
> *If thunder that day, then it signifieth a merrie year.'*

Palm Sunday is a fairly reliable prediction date, but Good Friday has an even better track record.

Author note – *over many years testing both, Good Friday does indeed have a better record.*

'Rain on Good Friday and Easter day,
A good year for grass and a bad year for hay.'

In other words, a wet year.

'Rainy Easter, a cheese year,'

The significant logic of this is simple, grass needs rain, good grass gives good milk yields, hence a wet year gives a good cheese year.

Authors note – *since the above are moveable feasts, many of the significant following days, be they saints days or other holy days, too are movable. i.e. Pentecost, Corpus Christi and Ascension day. It is therefore important to get these days and dates correct. There is a set formula for setting these dates and can be found in any reference library or from the internet. If taking such dates from a calendar or diary be additionally careful due to printing or submission errors. Accuracy is always the watchword.*

25th May
St Urban's Day

'St Urban gives the summer.'

It is certain that this day will give at least a fair indication of what the weather will be like, but with the warning that the signs can be ambiguous or a little optimistic.

15th June
St Vitus Day

> *'If St Vitus Day be rainy weather 'T'will rain for forty days together.'*

This can be a gloomy forecast for it encompasses St Swithin (15th July) the best known rain date of all, and being only 30 days ahead implicates 70 days of rain.

Uncle Offa is of the opinion that this should be 30 days only, covering the period between the two dates. If accepted then the 30 days is found to be more reliable. [*agreed by author*]

24th June
St John (the Baptist) Day also Quarter Day and Mid-summer day

> *'As the wind is on St John's day so it will be for three months.'*

> *'Mid-summer day rain spoils hay and grain.'*

Clearly a most important day with several entries found under the month of June. The longest day of the year, it is near the summer solstice (21st June), the day when the sun rises and sets at its most northerly points.

In the Druidical religion and in Witchery (Witchcraft) the most important ceremonies of the year are held then at places like Stonehenge.

15th July
St Swithun's Day

> *'St Swithin's Day if than dost rain*
> *Full forty days it will remain*
> *St Swithin's Day, if thou art fair*
> *Full forty days 'twill rain nae mair.'*

Or as Shakespeare put it

> *'If on St Swithin's feast the welkin lours*
> *And every pent house stream with hasty showers*
> *Twice twenty days shall clods their fleeces drain*
> *And wash the pavements with incessant rain.'*

This is the date for the sceptics for this day requires some thought. Most people in the UK are familiar with the significance of this day, and most of them, probably half, believe it. It may therefore be the only Day of Prediction known to the public at large.

St Swithin's Day is usually 'a bit of both,' day, half wet and half sunny. i.e. Sunny intervals and showers. Therefore St Swithin's Day is far from straightforward and it is better to be prudent and hedge your bets accordingly, and keep your reputation.

6th August
Transfiguration Day (of the Blessed Virgin Mary)

> *'As the weather is on the day of Transfiguration so it will be for the rest of the year.'*

This was first heard in Devon and Dorset, Uncle Offa is not an advocate [and neither is the author]. It is over ambitious, unreliable and out of rhythm with the other Days of Prediction, which occur at regular intervals throughout the year.

It is not considered as a true day of Prediction and therefore treated with extreme caution.

The author after 20 years of application found it most unreliable and now disregards this completely.

24th August
St Bartholomew's Day

> *'All the tears that St Swithin can cry St Bartelmy's mantle will wipe dry.'*

Note the affirmative 'will' and not 'may.' If St Swithin is wet then St Bartholomew will be dry – NB – this can be as much as three days either way!

If however St Swithin is dry, 'If Bartholomew's be fine and clear, then hope for a prosperous Autumn that year.'

Note also that the saw speaks of fine weather and says nothing about rain. After this day you should expect dull or fine weather, but not, as a general rule, much rain.

There are always exceptions to every rule and in this weather forecasting; exceptions are part of the norm.

29th September
St Michael's Day (Michaelmass) and Quarter Day

'As the wind is on St Michael's Day so 't'will be for three months.

A fairly dependable indication as to the direction of the wind.

It does however occur around the period of the Equinoxal gales which may give a false reading locally. If gales co-incide with this day, then wait a couple of days for a truer reading and forecast.

'A Quarter day, therefore a Wind day.'

11th November
St Martin's Day – Martinmass and Wind Day
(but not a Quarter Day)

The weather this day is said to fortell the weather for 3 months, furthermore where the wind blows on Martinmass Eve.

'Where the wind blows this day, there 't'will remain for the rest of winter.'

This is reinforced with the threat 'Wind NW on Martinmass and severe winter to come.'

This sounds gloomy, but it is the season for unsettled weather, with October and November crammed with weather signs affecting the oncoming winter and specific months in the New Year.

For example, St Clement's Day 23rd November, is said to give the weather for the following February

Author – *so does St Catherine on 25th November.*

Note well these sayings for they often add up to a very accurate picture.

NB Author's Note – *Living in Kent (western Kent bordering Surrey) in SE England, recent years have shown that incidence of the near continent and the weather there has a greater effect on this part of the UK, than the weather from the west.*

It is quite noticeable that the spring and summer periods are becoming warmer and dryer, but the winter and for the greater part, the weather extending well into late May, is much colder and dryer than previously.

The wind on this day is therefore arguable the most important single point for the winter in this area, since, if the wind is cold and strong from the east, or either side of this quadrant, then the perspective of a very cold, extremely cold at times, frosty or snowy winter is nearly guaranteed.

> *The persistence of the east wind however provides a 'cold blast' across the region at the very least until St Benedict (21st March) and in the last few years past St Urban (25th May) well into the second week of June. From the third week of June the south westerlies return.*
>
> *For my part, I am more than confident to place 100% faith in the wind direction for this day, and as been proven over the last three years has resulted in 100% accuracy.*

21st December
St Thomas's Day, Quarter day and Winter Solstice

> *'Look at the weather cock on St Thomas' Day, the wind will remain for three months.'*

There are those who consider that this day should actually read 'Christmas Day', but St Thomas does have a better track record.

There are a string of sayings pertinent to Christmas, but most of them hold up better if they were associated with the Solstice, which is of course, St Thomas's Day.

That ends the information concerning days of prediction that I have taken more or less, with the odd author's comment, from Uncle Offa. I make no excuse for this, since over 30 years I have found all his information; with the caveats he inserts, to be accurate and reliable.

I have tried other systems, but after exhaustive trialling none matched the above.

Quarter Days

There are four quarter days, similar, but not quite all the same as the old rent days.

The wind direction on these days is a most reliable indicator of the predominant direction of the wind up to the next quarter day, or approximately 90 days ahead. These winds indicate the prevailing direction for the whole period up to the next such day, and, it must be borne in mind that there will be periodic variations from time to time.

Quarter Days can be fairly described as 'wind days.'

To confuse matters a little more, there are also some days, not known as 'wind days' per se, November 11th – St Martin – being the best example, but such days are dealt with in detail under each monthly data sheet.

Quarter days

21st March (St Benedict and Equinox).

24th June (St John, Midsummer Day, longest day of the year).

29th September (Michaelmass)

21st December (St Thomas's, Winter equinox, shortest day of the year).

As a general rule the wind direction on 21st March will be easterly giving cold easterly winds up to at least 25th May (St Urban) and more likely (as in 2012 and 2013) well into the second week of June, when the direction changes to the south west bringing the warmer summer weather.

24th June will give south westerly warm winds, summer, and will last until 29th September, but stormy windy weather is more likely from 21st September (equinox) too.

29th September can be variable, by this I mean, some years it can be from the east giving very cold October and November weather, with frosts, it is however a dry wind which does not carry much moisture. It is preferable to have south westerly winds at this time to ensure a mild autumn (as in 2012). A cold wind this early can lead to a long cold winter.

21st December gives the winter wind and weather. If easterly then very cold (especially in May. However, some years it is from the south west (as in 2012) which then gives a wet and mild winter period, but this wind will change on 21st March. Which indicates why the winter 2012/2013 was so wet and mild, followed by a cold spring.

Over the years I consider that these wind dates are highly reliable and as such will always outweigh any official meteorological forecasts. This may cause some eyebrows to rise – just pause and consider the latest 'metspeak – jet streams,' compare the prevalence of these conditions to the quarter day wind direction. You may be surprised.

Met Office Stormy and Quiet Periods and Buchan Warm and Cool Periods

Met Office (UK) stormy and quiet periods

The UK Met office have periods through the year, that they classify as 'Stormy' or 'Quiet' periods, defined as period when storms are more than likely to occur, or periods of calm benign weather will reign supreme. Such period are quite accurate too, and again, when used in conjunction with other data help complete the monthly jig-saw to complete the picture.

Stormy Periods

5th – 17th January
25–31st January
24th–28th(29th) February
24th October to 13th November
24th November to 14th December
25th–31st December.

Quiet Periods

18th–24th January
1st–17th September
16th–20th October
15th–21st November.

It is interesting to note that when these dates are inserted onto the monthly spreadsheet the correlation between the weather becomes quite apparent.

Buchan Cold and Warm periods

In the late 19th century a Scottish Meteorologist named Alexander Buchan, working from Edinburgh, deducted that at certain fixed times of the year the average temperature was higher (warmer) or lower (colder) than the norm. He therefore worked out these periods and they are established as Buchan Periods. Whilst they refer to Edinburgh, I have been using them for the last 40 years, and for the greater part they are remarkably accurate, even here in Kent, they are therefore part of the methodology I use.

The Cold Periods

7th–14th February
11th–14th April
9th–14th May
29th June to 4th July:
6th–13th November.

The Warm periods

13th–15th July
12th–15th August
3rd–14th December.

Concerning the cold periods, the April dates coincide with the Blackthorn winter; the May dates with the Ice-Maidens and the June period with Wimbledon Tennis fortnight.

Concerning the warm periods the July period covers the 14th July that is considered by many to be one of the consistently hottest days of the year, and the same for the August period too, quite often the hottest period of the year.

The Moon

The Moon goes through various phases:

NEW MOON

CRESCENT/WAXING MOON

FIRST QUARTER

WAXING GIBBOUS

FULL MOON

WANING GIBBOUS

LAST QUARTER

WANING CRESCENT

A fuller description of each follows.

The phases of the moon are caused by the positions of the Earth, Moon and Sun. The tides are affected by these positions too.

The Earth revolves around the sun taking a whole year to do so, and because the earth rotates we have day and night, each rotation takes 24 hours. The night sky shows when Earth faces away from the Sun.

The Moon produces no light of its own, it reflects the sunlight. Therefore at any one time there is a dark side and a light side on the Moon, as on Earth.

74

We see the Moon from earth and as the Moon orbits the earth, its position with the Sun changes, hence we get various phases of the Moon.

The Moon orbits the Earth anti-clockwise, which is the same direction as the earth's spin and Earth's orbit.

The NEW MOON occurs when the Moon is directly on the Sun side of the Earth; the Moon is 'New' when it is between Earth and the Sun. The NEW MOON rises and sets along with the Sun at about the same time, and has its shadowed face towards Earth.

After a few days the Moon has moved and a part of the Moon becomes illuminated by the sunlight producing a WAXING CRESCENT MOON soon after sunset. A WAXING CRESCENT MOON also occurs during the opposite part of its orbit, before sunset in the east. Careful observation on a clear night will reveal that the rest of the moon is very dimly lit; this is caused by sunlight reflecting off the Earth and shining on the Moon and reflecting back to Earth, this light is called Earthshine.

The Moon now moves into a right angle position with the Earth, a half-moon, but it is called commonly the FIRST QUARTER, there is another quarter illuminated on the far side of the Moon, and within a few days becomes WAXING GIBBOUS MOON. As the moon goes from new to full it is called 'waxing;' because it is gibbous, which is more than a quarter but less than full and waxing, which means it becomes more illuminated each night.

A FULL MOON is one that is fully illuminated by the Sun and follows the previous moon. Due to its positioning a FULL MOON rises in the east at about the same time as the sun sets in the west. A FULL MOON is very bright, some being brighter than others (Super moons) which make it very difficult to see detail in the night sky.

The FULL MOON now starts to wane, an old word that means diminish/decline, and after the FULL MOON the Moon now becomes a WANING GIBBOUS MOON, gibbous since it is more than a quarter, but less than full, and waning as it declines.

This WANING GIBBOUS MOON continues to wane as it continues its orbit and becomes a LAST QUARTER MOON, and again is at a right angle to the Earth-Sun line.

As the nights pass the Moon continues to wane and produces an OLD MOON, which is another (WANING) CRESCENT MOON, but it is the opposite side that is illuminated as a crescent.

The cycle is now completed and starts again back to the NEW MOON.

The above gives a brief description of the phases of the Moon. There are several in-depth and more comprehensive features to be found on the internet.

The Moon and Weather Lore

During the hours of research I did before settling down and encompassing all the data into some sort of order, I came across in the archives at Canterbury Cathedral dating from about 1200 AD, a chart, that split the day into 2 hour segments commencing midnight through the following 24 hours. Beside each two hour slot was a weather condition (fair; rainy etc). The chart was divided into summer and winter too.

With BST here in the UK I decided to use winter as commencing on 1st October and ending 14th April. Summer therefore 15th April until 30th September.

I use the http://www.timeanddate.com website to pinpoint

my exact location, then obtain the moon phase time from the appropriate drop down menu provided; this time and date is then checked against the relevant moon time and the weather for that phase is given. It must remembered to add the 1 hour BST after the commencement of BST here in the UK – and to resume to the original times at the conclusion of BST.

However the identical chart was also found at Rochester Cathedral archives dating form the late 1200 ad period, therefore with two such findings I decided that it was good enough to incorporate into my methodology – and it is now one of the main parts of the methodology. It must have worked in 1200 ad – and, as far as I am concerned it works extremely well now.

Both the summer and winter tables appear below.

Over many years experience I will give an indication as to what certain words show;

In Summer

Fair = dry bright sunny warm with no wind
Cold and showers = just that at any place and at any time
Changeable = anything and everything
Rain = at any time and at any place but more persistent than
    showers.

In Winter

Fair and mild = dry sunny calm and bright
Fair and frosty = cold frosty nights but cold dry sunny calm
    days
Rain or snow = rain, but if cold enough then snow.

If, the New Moon, First Quarter, Full Moon or last Quarter occur between the following hours, the weather here stated below is said to occur.

In Summer

0000–0200hrs	Fair
0200–0400hrs	Cold and showers
0400–0600hrs	Rain
0600–0800hrs	Wind and rain
0800–1000hrs	Changeable
1000–1200hrs	Frequent showers
1200–1400hrs	Very rainy
1400–1600hrs	Changeable
1600–1800hrs	Rain
1800–2000hrs	Fair if NW Wind (NW winds are uncommon in summer)
22000–2200hrs	Rainy – if wind S or SW (more likely summer direction)
2200–2400hrs	Fair.

In Winter

0000–0200hrs	Frost – unless wind SW (SW winds uncommon in winter)
0200–0400hrs	Snowy and stormy
0400–0600hrs	Rain
0600–0800hrs	Stormy
0800–1000hrs	Cold rain if wind westerly
1000–1200hrs	Cold and high winds
1200–1400hrs	Snow and rain
1400–1600hrs	Fair and mild
1600–1800hrs	Fair

1800–2000hrs	Fair and frosty if wind NE or N
2000–2200hrs	Rain or snow if winds S or SW
2200–2400hrs	Fair and frosty.

Full Moon Names and Their Meanings

Full Moon names date back to Native Americans, of what is now the northern and eastern United States. The tribes kept track of the seasons by giving distinctive names to each recurring full moon. Their names were applied to the whole month in which occurred. There was some variation in Moon names, but in general the same ones were current throughout the Algonquin tribes from New England to Lake Superior. European settlers followed that custom and created some of their own names. Since the lunar month is only 29 days long on the average, the Full Moon dates shift from year to year. Here is the Farmers Almanac's list of the Full Moon names.

Full Wolf Moon

JANUARY amid the cold deep snows of mid-winter the wolf packs howled hungrily outside Indian villages. Thus the name for January's full Moon. Sometimes it was also referred to as the Old Moon, or the Moon after Yule. Some called it the Full Snow Moon, but most tribes applied that name to the next Moon.

Full Snow Moon

FEBRUARY since the heaviest snow usually falls during this month, native tribes of the north and east most often called February's full Moon the Full Snow Moon. Some tribes also referred to this moon as the Full Hunger Moon, since harsh weather conditions in their areas made hunting very difficult.

Full Worm Moon

MARCH as the temperature begins to warm and the ground begins to thaw, earthworm casts appear, heralding the return of the robins. The more northerly tribes knew this Moon as the Full Crow Moon, when the cawing of the crows signalled the end of the winter; or the Full Crusted Moon because the snow cover becomes crusted from thawing by day and freezing at night. The Full Sap Moon, marking the time of tapping maple trees, is another variation. To the settlers, it was known as the Lenten Moon and was considered to be the last full moon of winter.

Full Moon Pink

APRIL this name came from the herb moss pink, or wild ground phlox, which is one of the earliest widespread flowers of the spring. Other names for this month's celestial body include the Full Sprouting Grass Moon, the Egg Moon, and among celestial tribes the Full Fish Moon, because this was the time that the shad swam upstream to spawn.

Full Flower Moon

MAY in most areas, flowers are most abundant everywhere during this time. Thus, the name of the moon. Other names include the Full Corn Planting Moon. Or the Milk Moon

Full Strawberry Moon

JUNE this name was universal to every Algonquin tribe. However, in Europe they called it the Rose Moon. Also because of the relatively short season for harvesting strawberries comes each year during the month of June…so the full Moon that occurs during that month was christened for the strawberry.

The Full Buck Moon

JULY is normally the month when the new antlers of the buck deer push out of their foreheads in coatings of velvety fur. It was also often called the Full Thunder Moon, for that reason that the thunderstorms are most frequent during this time. Another name for this month's Moon was the Full Hay Moon.

Full Sturgeon Moon

AUGUST the fishing tribes are given credit for the naming of this Moon, since sturgeon, a large fish of the Great Lakes and other bodies of water, were most readily caught during this month. A few tribes knew it as the Full Red Moon because, as the Moon rises, it appears reddish through any sultry haze. It was also called the Green Corn Moon of Grain Moon.

Full Corn Moon or Full Harvest Moon

SEPTEMBER this full moon's name is attributed to Native Americans because it marked when corn was supposed to be harvested. Most often the September full moon is actually the Harvest Moon, that is the moon that occurs closest to the autumn equinox. In two years out of three, the Harvest Moon comes in September, but in some years it occurs in October. At the peak of harvest, farmers can work late into the night by the light of this moon. Usually the Full Moon rises an average of 50 minutes later each night, but for the few nights around the Harvest Moon, the Moon seems to rise at nearly the same time each night; just 25 to 30 minutes across the U.S. and only 102 to 20 minutes later for much of Canada and Europe. Corn, pumpkins, squash, beans and wild rice the chief Indian staples are now ready for gathering.

Full Hunters Moon or Full Harvest Moon

OCTOBER this Full Moon is often referred to as the Full Hunters Moon, Blood Moon or Sanguine Moon. Many moons ago, Native Americans named this bright moon for obvious reasons. The leaves falling from the trees, the deer are fattened, and it's time to begin storing meat for the long winter ahead. Because the fields are traditionally reaped in late September or early October hunters could easily see fox and other animals that come out to glean from the fallen grains. Probably because of the threat of winter looming close, the Hunter's Moon is generally accorded with special honour, historically serving as an important feast day in both Western Europe and among many Native Tribes.

Full Beaver Moon

NOVEMBER this was the time to set beaver traps before the swamps froze, to ensure a supply of warm winter furs. Another interpretation suggests that the name Full Beaver Moon comes from the fact that the beavers are now actively preparing for winter. It is also sometimes referred to as the Frosty Moon.

The Full Cold Moon or The Full Long Nights Moon

DECEMBER during this month the winter cold fastens its grip, and nights are at their longest and darkest. It is also sometimes called the Moon before the Yule. The term Long Night Moon is a doubly appropriate name because the midwinter night is indeed long, and because the Moon is above the horizon for a long time. The midwinter full Moon has a high trajectory across the sky because it is opposite a low sun.

Moon names

Full moons come, full moons go,
Softening nights with their silver glow
They pass in silence
All untamed
But as they travel
They are named.

Saints Days, other Days and Non Holy Days

The main Christian holy days have been covered previously, as have Days of Prediction and Quarter days. However there are also some days, that fall outside these categories, that nevertheless, still have an important place in the methodology, be they informative, as for flowering plants, for the collection of fruits as St Filbert, the day when Filbert nuts are harvested, or even days of celebration such a Chestnut Sunday, Burns Night, St David's day. Some days celebrate local festivals such St Padarn in Cornwall. However it is for local practices whether such days are entered onto a spreadsheet for each month.

There are also some Holy days that do not get a mention under other headings, such as Annunciation day of the Blessed Virgin Mary or Holy Rood day.

All the above manage to get a mention on each monthly data sheet and also the spreadsheet, one has brief details (spreadsheet) the other has fuller details (data sheet), one therefore compliments the other.

Supermoons, Perigee and Apogee, Equinox, Eclipses and Meteorological Seasons

Super-moon

A Super-moon, is a moon that is much larger and brighter than the average moon.

The terminology was defined in 1979 by Richard Nolle the astrologer, as a new or full moon which occurs with the Moon at or near (within 90%) its closest approach to earth in a given orbit (perigee). In short, Earth, Moon and Sun are all in a line, with the moon at its nearest approach to earth.

Richard Nolle also argues that with +/– 3 days of a supermoon, the earth is more subject to natural disasters such as earthquakes and volcanic activity because of the Moon's increased gravitational force (raised by 18%).

A full moon at perigee is 12% larger and brighter than an average full moon.

When allied to the previous column of Apogee and Perigee dates and times, the inclusion of Supermoon dates becomes significant, and thus the entry.

Again this was not within the knowledge of persons in former times, but I consider this information to be important enough to enter, even as just a precautionary note, to my charts.

It is however worth noting that numerous comments, with on-going enquiries and research still in hand, as to what effect the supermoon at the time had on the 2011 Japanese earthquake.

To obtain detailed information concerning pending Supermoons just search the internet. However a very good and reliable site: www.timeanddate.com/calendar.html Will give you moon phases. Eclipse, sunrise, sunset, apogee and perigee data too.

Perigee and Apogee

A Perigee is when the moon is nearest the earth.

An Apogee is when the moon is furthest from the earth.

If a Perigee occurs within 24 hours of a full moon, there is a proven correlation that the likelihood of a major natural disaster occurring at this period is raised 100%.

An example is high tide at full moon – a spring tide even, combined with excessive water from heavy rains, and/or the surge of water (North sea surge) all combining together to cause a major flood – it is of note the Christmas Tsunami in the Pacific was on such a date, and there are numerous other such natural disasters that all fit into this category.

Another more recent example is Hurricane Sandy that devastated parts of the New York hinterland in 2012.

Therefore a Perigee at the time of a full moon is an extreme warning that should be heeded, and the preponderance for a major natural disaster, be it earthquake, tsunami, acute flooding, volcano eruption etc increases by 100%. Those within tidal areas should be particularly aware.

However, it is also possible to have such a natural catastrophe adjacent to an Apogee, when the full moon is present and the tides are high, as in the 'Sandy' hurricane in the NE USA and the Caribbean.

Not generally acknowledged but these two events, Apogee and Perigee, should be treated with the utmost respect, especially when all the other parameters fall into place.

Perigee and Apogee dates and times can be obtained from the internet, the Official NASA and US Navy sites being proven reliable sources. Please avoid the astrology sites for these dates.

Again a word of caution here when using such data, please ensure your exact position (as in moon data) is correct.

However a very good and reliable site: www.timeanddate. com/calendar/moonphases.html
Will give you Moon Phases. Eclipse, Sunrise, Sunset, Apogee and Perigee data too.

Equinoxes

There are four such days in the year and are closely allied to Quarter Days, they are:

21st March – Spring or vernal equinox.
21st June – summer equinox (around the longest day of the year).
21st September (but subject to some slight variation) – autumn equinox.
21st December – winter equinox – shortest day of the year.

Eclipses

Eclipses of the sun (solar) or moon (lunar) also play their part in the methodology.

These occurrences are noted in the monthly data sheets as they occur.

Sometimes too, what is known as a Super-moon also occurs during such an event, a Super-moon being when the moon appears to be larger, clearer or more radiant than normal.

Meteorological seasons

The Met Office UK sets the seasons of the year as follows:

Spring = 1st March to 31st May.
Summer = 1st June to 31st August.
Autumn = 1st September to 30th November.
Winter = 1st December to 28th February.

Using Nature and Natures Signs of What Lies Ahead

This is a truly vast subject and I can only but scratch the surface, but having said that I can give some indications of what to look and see.

Every one looks but less than 1% actually see. By this I mean, I will walk into any countryside or rural situation and immediately identify what trees, shrubs, bushes, grasses, wild flowers, birds or animals are, or are likely to be present; the state of the plants, flowers trees or shrubs will tell me the season of the year, and, from this I can recognise what is likely to come. Nature is always working at least one growing season ahead (90 days), in some cases it is 180 days ahead. A classic example is the sun shining at Christmas day (the twelfth month) if the sun shines this day then it fortells the month of May(fifth month-no killer frosts for the fruit blossoms), the summer months of July (seventh month) and August (eighth month) will be fortuitous for the fruit and grain harvest. If the grass is not growing on the 1st January then there will be just one hay harvest in June (six months hence).

In spring, does the blossom come first or the flower first on the blackthorn and hawthorn? What date did the crocus appear (14th February), what day did the snowdrop appear (2nd February). How early was the lesser celandine? What day did the cuckoo plant appear (17th April) – why cuckoo plant? The cuckoo plant heralds within 36 hours the arrival of the first cuckoo, followed by the nightingale and then the martins.

In summer, how high and in what quantity the hogweed, the higher they grow then the harder the ground in winter, be it frozen, flooded or covered in snow; the teasels and burdock the same, all being food for the finches and smaller birds.

In autumn, how many sloes, spindle, hawthorn berries, rose hips or elder berries, the stock winter foods for the incoming migratory birds from the arctic. How many acorns, sycamore seeds, ash seeds, sorbus berries, yew, ivy and holly berries, more food for the winter birds.

In winter, how early did the robin stake out its territory in the back garden adjacent to the back door – where the food is? The earlier it stakes its claim the longer colder and harder the forthcoming winter. How thick are the onion skins of the English onions – the thicker the skin the harder the winter. How many stinging nettles in the roadside verges – the more nettles the better for the tortoiseshell butterfly next spring, since that is where they lay their eggs for the spring. How thick and early do the sheep and horses start to grow their winter coats, the cattle the same, all signs of a long hard winter. How many jays burying acorns for retrieval later? How many squirrels hoarding nuts and building nests in safe places in the trees?

If you look you actually can see. The Ivy bush, a weed that encompasses walls and trees, yet vital for the small birds, the tits, wren robin, sparrows; the ivy fruits are the sole nectar plants of the winter, thereby attracting such insects as there are; the leaves are waterproof and windproof. The leaves also collect water from rain on the outside, therefore the small birds have a windproof, waterproof home, with food and water present too.

The mighty oak tree not only provides acorns for birds, deer and other creatures, but if the winter is to be hard, cold and long, will retain its leaves for the winter, thereby giving some windproof cover for birds – as does the copper beech and beech, the latter providing beech nuts too.

There are plenty of good reading books to increase your knowledge of such wonderful things, the website has plenty of such suggested good literature to help you.

Do not disregard nature, nature is never wrong, it gives warning in February and March of likely drought ahead, as in July and August 2016 in the SE, all again six months ahead; it never fails to look after its own. Open your eyes, look and see what there is out there, boundless knowledge too.

All small insignificant things in themselves but when collated with everything else all building to produce a vivid, enlightening, wonderful picture of what is to come.

Flowers of the Month

A list of wild flowers and their flowering dates, which indicate too how far in advance or how far behind the seasons are:

February 2nd .... Snowdrop
February 14th .... Crocus
March 1st .... Daffodil
April 11th–14th .... Blackthorn
April 17th .... Lady's Smock
April 23rd .... Harebell
May 3rd .... Crowfoot
May 22nd .... Dandelion picking East Anglia

June 11th .... Ragged Robin
June 24th .... Scarlet Lynchis
July 14th .... Lavender harvest
July 15th .... Lily flowering
July 20th .... Poppy day
July 22nd .... Rose flowering
August 1st .... Camomile
August 18th .... Cob/Filbert nut harvest
August 24th .... Sunflower
September 14th .... Passion flower
September 29th .... Michaelmass daisy
November 25th .... Laurel tree flowers
December 25th .... Holly and Ivy

Trees of each Month

24/12 to 20/1 .... Birch
21/1 to 17/2 .... Rowan
18/2 to 17/3 .... Ash
18/3 to 14/4 .... Alder
15/4 to 12/5 .... Willow
13/5/ to 9/6 .... Hawthorn
10/6 to 7/7 .... Oak
8/7 to 4/8 .... Holly
5/8 to 1/9 .... Hazel
2/9 to 29/9 .... Vine
30/9 to 27/10 .... Ivy
28/10 to 23/11 .... Reed
24/11 to 23/12 .... Elder

Some Bird Notes

We all see birds everyday, but what do we actually see?

In summer the martins, swallows and swifts all fly high in the blue summer skies, why? Because the air pressure is high then the insects and their food is also high, therefore as they acrobatically swoop, glide, tumble and turn they are feeding in the sky.

So why then on a poor weather day, with cloud, do they fly low sometimes below knee height skimming over the ground? This is because the air pressure is low, a sign of inclement weather, and as such the insects are forced lower, therefore the birds fly lower for food.

If it going to a windy year, in early spring when the rook and crows build their nests high in the larger trees (oak, elm) they will build them in the nearest branch cleft to the top, not at the top, since building them in a cleft will protect the nest better when the high winds arrive.

The green woodpecker is a ground feeding bird, eating worms and grubs from the soil. The other members of the wood pecker family are tree living birds and gain their food from the bark and branches of trees – hence the 'drilling' noises you hear walking in woodland.

The ground feeding birds, wagtails, blackbirds, thrushes, robins, sparrows will be seen grubbing out beneath hedges and low plants for food, though in winter and early spring the blackbirds will be seen higher in the bushes eating berries.

The jay, a woodland bird collects and buries acorns in season, and later when necessary will return and dig up these acorns to eat. Woodland birds, such as the jay, wood pigeon, woodpecker have shorter wings enabling them to navigate the trees better.

Certain birds arrive more or less at the same time each year, April 17th is the arrival times for the cuckoo, the nightingale soon follows and then the martins and swallows. Soon after this in early May the song birds arrive, but the swifts do not appear until late May and fly off again at the latest mid-July. The cuckoo departs by mid-July too having deposited its sole egg in another bird's nest, it leaves the new cuckoo to find its own way back to Africa where it over-winters. The martins and swallows depart normally late August, though at times do stay longer, for west Africa. The smaller song birds having departed mid August for warmer climes too.

There is a perceptibly quiet period from early September to mid-October when the countryside is devoid of song birds and song sounds; just the raucous cries of the crow family, the squabbling of the starlings, the early territory staking song of the robin and the twitterings of the tits and gold finches are common. The wood peckers too are quite distinctive as is the cooing of the pigeon family.

However towards the end of October the arrival of the winter migrants, the fieldfare, redwing, arctic starling, brambling liven the skies as these flocks of birds flit from feeding source to feeding source through the trees eating berries hips and haws as they go – a little from each source with no greed, eking out the valuable food sources. These are accompanied by the migratory ducks, mallard, gadwall, teal, scoter, tufted and many more, plus if the winter is to be really long cold and hard, besides the normal migrants greylag, Canada and white fronted geese, the pink-footed, brent and barnacle geese also make an appearance. All these ducks and geese stay until weather conditions are suitable for them to fly off north again, normally at the end of March into the first week of April.

There is normally a gap of a couple of weeks between the departure of the winter migrants to the north, and the arrival of the migrants from the south.

A sure sign of a hard winter to come is the early arrival of waxwings from the near continent, and also too if food sources are scarce on the continent too, jays come for the acorns. Mallard and gadwall ducks too will increase in numbers, plus too the odd mute swan and occasional bewick swan.

Constructing a Monthly Data Sheet

For demonstration purposes this is the data sheet for October 2016.

You will see the moon phases and the weather for that phase. Highest spring tides; Perigee and apogee dates and times – and this time a danger warning. The Met Office Stormy and quiet periods plus the Buchan warm and cooler periods too. No Day of Prediction. The moon name and trees of the month included. Therefore everything discussed in previous chapters now starts to be collated into a bulletin.

There then follows the daily events where appropriate.

EXAMPLE : OCTOBER 2016

NEW MOON = 1st @ 0113hrs = FROST AND

30th @ 1739hrs = FAIR

1ST QUARTER MOON = 9th @ 0535hrs = RAIN

FULL MOON 16th @ 0525hrs = RAIN

LAST QUARTER MOON 22nD @ 2016hrs = RAIN/SNOW

DOP = NONE THIS MONTH

HIGHEST SPRING TIDES 16th TO 21st

APOGEE 4th @ 1103hrs, AND 31st @ 1930hrs

PERIGEE 16th @ 2337hrs

DANGER WARNING: FULL MOON + PERIGEE + HIGHEST SPRING TIDES

16th TO 21st EXPECT SEVERE WEATHER PROBLEMS

3rd   Day of celebration after wine harvest

4th   Apogee @ 1103hrs

11th   Vinalia Day
        New wine testing day. Apogee 14.18hrs

16th   Gallas
        see notes for 29th September. PERIGEE @ 2337hrs.

18th   St Luke
        St Luke's little summer is a fine day (4 days to a
        week of lovely weather)

28th   St Simon and St Jude
       Marks the end limit of St Luke's little summer.
       A rainy day. On St Jude's day the oxen may play
       (end of heavy farm work).
30th   BST ENDS
31st   Hallowtide
       If ducks swim at Hallowtide, at Christmas the same
       ducks will slide. The onset of winter and darker time
       of the year. Apogee @ 1930hrs

Met Office notes

16th to 19th Quiet period.
24th to 13th November a stormy period.

Buchan notes

None.

To the above is now added all the detailed data, saws/sayings
and features of this month and also in some cases for the following months too. This is a compilation of of the original
50,000 saws/sayings I originally collected, reducing to some
5,000. All the saws here are tried, tested and proven, all refer
to this month of October.

Finally an indication of rainfall and temperatures at this
site is added (with a suitable caveat). It is hoped that such
monthly data will assist any reader to be able in due course
to make a reasonable assessment of what weather is to come,
the signs and later the effects.

General Notes and Comments

- The Golden month – star of the weather prophets year.

- The month with more weather signs than any month, but it has no day of prediction.

- All October predictions look forward well into December and the New Year.

- October has 19/21 fine days, maybe over-optimistic, but usually more fine than rough.

- October forecast signs fit well with days of prediction, and should be taken seriously. Best reputation for long range forecasts.

- St Luke usually gives 4 days to a week of lovely weather. (very true) He does however sometimes arrive five days late!

- One can reasonably expect a warm period between mid-September and mid-November.

- Feast of St Simon and St Jude signals the start of a very stormy period, and the end of St Likes summer. It is also claimed there is never a year without rain this day.

- Abundance of acorns, dead nettles and thick onion skins in October indicate a hard winter.

- Heavy crop of haw-berries and beech nuts indicates a bad winter to come.

- 31st – Halloween. Has a reputation for being a quiet night.

- The garden month – expect downpours of rain.

- For every October fog there will be snow in winter, heavy or light according to the fog. Most reliable indeed.

- Full moon in October without frost, no frost till full moon in November. (a golden rule)

- If the October moon is born with the points up, the month will be dry. If down, wet. (the old saying being that a moon on its back catches the rain – a moon on its side cannot catch the rain)

- If during leaf-fall in October many leaves remain hanging, a frosty winter with much snow will follow. (very true)

- If in October leaves till hold, the coming winter will be cold (yes).

- Late leaf fall, hard in New Year, (true)

- If Oak bears its leaves in October there will be a hard winter. [very reliable]

- If in the fall of leaves many of them wither on the boughs and hang there, a frosty winter and much snow will follow. (proven yes)

- If foxes bark much in October they are calling up great falls of snow. (true even in cities)

- (If no foxes or hares in your district watch the sheep. If they cluster together and move slowly, it is a sure sign of snow). Yes – proven with sheep.

- If the hare wears a thick coat in October, he shows his wisdom. (lay in a good stock of fuel)

- When owls hunt in daylight, expect a hard winter.

- If squirrels early mass their hoard, expect a winter like a sword.

- When birds and badgers are fat in October, you may expect a cold winter.

- If there is snow and frost in October, January will be mild.

- If October brings much frost and rain, then January and February will be mild.

- Windy October, dry January; warm October, cold February.

- If late October and early November are warm and rainy there is a better chance that January and February will be cold and frosty. (Proven from local records)

- October wet, March dry. [yes if October above average, March will be below average]

- October cold, March cold (is more likely from local records). October warm, March colder than average (proven from local records)

- The last week in October is the wettest of the year in southern England and the chances of a dry day on the 28th is minimal. [official averages]

- Observe the first heavy fog in August and expect a hard frost the same day in October. [check readings]

- Much rain in October, much wind/rain in December.

- When it freezes and snows in October, January will bring mild weather, but if it is thunder and lightning, the weather will resemble April in temper.

- If October brings heavy frosts and winds, then January and February will be mild.

- Redwings arrive mid-October and Fieldfares the end of October.

- In October dung your field and your land its wealth shall yield.

- The end of summer -leaves turn gold and fall, the chills of autumn herald the onset of winter.

- Wine harvest vintage month.

- Time of first frosts and final harvest. The greater the harvest, the greater the frost and snow the following winter.

The full moon this month is called the HUNTER'S MOON.

The tree of the month up to 27th is the IVY, thereafter the REED.

Monthly averages for
Edenbridge (using 1981–2010 figures)

Mean Max:	16C
Mean Min:	6.5C
Mean Avg:	11.25C
Rainfall:	92.9mm
Sunshine:	131.2hrs (day = 4.23hrs)

Whilst I appreciate the above are local figures, it will be an indication of what the averages are, and, of course there will be local variations. Such variations can be found by trawling the various weather websites, or by using the superb data found in the Climatologists Observers Link website.

The following figures are for the average temperature at 12 noon and again at 4pm, taken at the beginning and again at the end of the month.

	12 noon	4pm
1st	16C	17C
31st	11.8C	11.3C

From the above you can now see in considerable detail what to reasonable expect in October; which migratory birds will arrive from the arctic regions. What the significance is of acorns. How information from this month gives information for months ahead, it is therefore, an on-going daily process 'One day telleth another – Psalms 19.2'

This collection is collated from some 40 different tried, tested and proven sources and helps show how the methodology then produces the prediction, and why.

How the monthly data sheet and spreadsheet are assembled

In order to indicate how a monthly prediction/forecast looks when completed I have attached the complete entry for October 2016.

You will see how some of the entries interact with future dates and future weather; at the same time it gives an indication of how each of the previous matters here go into the production of one month.

Note too how the Met Office stormy periods dovetail perfectly with the stormy moons.

From the data that occurs during the month a separate log is kept for each future month, up to a year ahead, and the data noted. To state therefore that, for example, Spring 2016 would be cold and wet, June would be very wet, and that the summer as such, would appear in the last two weeks of July 2016 and well into the first 12 days of August, I needed four separate unconnected reliable and proven facts, that I could check and verify (from previously collected data), when the four facts all agreed then I make the pronouncement/prediction/forecast. Such pronouncements contain no technological input; everything is gathered from the same sources as our fore-fathers had. It worked for them, and, as I am now proving, works very well for me now.

I adopt a ruling, a set of parameters, that I must have four separate unconnected pieces of data, checked and verified for each affirmative entry. There are some exceptions to this rule when there are three really significant pieces of data; anything less than three is excluded.

I must always follow the trail the data produces, however 'off the wall' [like four consecutive rain moons in September 2016] it may appear, for as soon as I deviate, the methodology is useless and worthless. So to state in January 2016 that the summer would appear in the last two weeks of July 2016 was not an act of faith, it was based on solid fact that I checked, verified and was proven reliable.

Similarly to state that June 2016 would be both damp and cold was equally checked verified and proven. You will find on certain current 'flow-charts' that the 'if....then' occur; similarly there are such similarities with weather, and , even in the 1200 AD period these were used to great effect; they were active then just as they are active now; the theory of computerisation was forming in the 1200 AD period!

I am often asked 'how do you know with such certainty?' – the simple answer is that I have been doing this for many years now, and, as the methodology improves – and it is now as good as I can get it – the resultant predictions improve; which does not by any means say that I am infallible, I am not, and never claim to be perfect; but, if it goes badly wrong, then I retrace all the footsteps and invariably I find I have misread or misinterpreted a small but vital (in hindsight) detail.

So, I aim for a minimum accuracy of 90% (working at least 90 days in advance) as far as I am able, sometimes I attain the magic 100%, but with human error nothing is infallible either.

Since this book, and the website, without any disrespect to the reader, the aim is to describe in simple non-technical terms – which is why space has been given to explaining, eg, Days of Prediction, Quarter days etc elsewhere in the text, it is written by a Dummy – for Dummies – there is a highly successful book publisher who uses this title and therefore I borrow from those volumes.

Each website monthly entry comes in four parts, the first being a preamble – which recaps from the previous month, highlights major events for the coming month; makes comments upon press or national newspaper articles or claims. Sometimes too, since this is a democracy, I have 'tick or two,' about a comment adverse or other wise occurring in the month. It is never disrespectful, contentious maybe, but we live in a free democracy – you can always turn the 'off' switch.

The second part is the data sheet as explained above, as quite self-explanatory.

Next is the simple spreadsheet, where everything noted in detail on the previous data sheet is shown in date form simply on the sheet. It does however highlight any major weather problems, like flooding dangers at such times.

Finally the HH Lamb sheet. To show/corroborate just how the methodology works, and also how well it works, I drew up a second spreadsheet where I encapsulated academic comments and readings taken over many years by established meteorological experts in their fields for each month. Each month shows what these academics found day by day, and, as will be seen, their results are quite similar; such similarities can then be used against the previous spreadsheet to see just how accurate the methodology is;a kind of verification for want of a better word.

I have appended the whole year January to December 2016 here of the datasheet entries, where the reader can see just how one month will indicate the future weather of another month.

Assembling the Website Monthly Spreadsheet

The website monthly spreadsheet is designed as a quick and easy reference point for the reader, where a quick glance for any day of the month will tell you in brief what you need to know. More detailed data can be found on the larger comprehensive data sheet.

The spreadsheet is divided into columns with the date and days on the left, and running across the sheet from left to right showing the moon phase, weather, Day of Prediction, Quarter day, Holy Day, Saint or other day, Apogee or Perigee, Met office stormy or quiet period, Buchan period, Equinox/Eclipse/Super-moon, highest tides.

		Moon	*Weather*	DoP	OCTOBER	2016
		Moon	*Weather*	DoP	Saint/Holy	Other
					Day	day
1	S	NEW	*frost*			
2	S					
3	M					
4	T					
5	W					
6	T					
7	F					
8	S					
9	S	1stQ	*rain*			
10	M					
11	T					Vinalia day
12	W					
13	T					
14	F					
15	S					
16	S	FULL	*rain*		DANGER	
17	M				PERIOD	
18	T				15th to	St Luke
19	W				20th	
20	T					
21	F					
22	S	LQ	*rain/snow*			
23	S					
24	M					
25	T					
26	W					
27	T					
28	F					St Simon/St Jude
29	S					
30	S	NEW	*fair*		BST ENDS	
31	M					Halloween

Quarter day	Apogee Perigee	Met Off Stormy/quiet	Buchan warm/cool	Super - Moon	Highest tides
	apogee 1103hrs				
	perigee 2337hrs	quiet			highest
		16th			tides
		to			16th
		20th			to
		"			21st
		stormy			
		24th			
		to			
		13 Nov			
	apogee 1930hrs	121			

Therefore everything discussed in this book is shown in easy format.

Every now and then the methodology, now tried, tested and proven after many years of testing, shows up in stark detail, a danger point. This more often than not occurs when the highest tides, full moon and perigee all coincide within the 36 hour window, such data is then highlighted as such and appropriate warnings or advice is given in the main text of the website and/or in the preamble. It is to forewarn and advise and is the result of the methodology. It is as good as I can get it.

Some Weather Day Peculiarities or 'Dead Certs'

There are throughout the year, some days that can be regularly be expected to be what I call 'dead certs,' by this I indicate that year in year out, be they a fixed date or movable date then the resulting weather will always be the same.

I start with the four quarter days, 21st March, 24th June, 29th September and 21st December. Where the wind blows on each of these days WILL BE the predominant wind direction for the next 90 days until the next such quarter day. Equally the wind direction on the 24th June will be from the SW – a warm summer air stream giving us summer.

September 29th can be variable, most times it remains from the SW, but every now and then it becomes a N or NE wind, blowing form those segments and bringing with it, dry cold air from the near continent.

The December 21st wind too cannot, even though it is winter, be relied upon to be a cold wind, 2015 was a classic example that gave a really warm winter.

21st March however has in recent years been a cold E wind veering to the N at times, hence the raw cold springs of 2014 to 2016.

There are however a couple of anomalies to the above. The 11th November (St Martin – St Martin's little summer, a short period of 3 days or so fine dry bright weather) is a 'wind' day, where the wind blows this day will stay as the predominant wind direction until the 2nd February (Candlemass), in other words, gives the winter wind. Which then brings us to that 2nd February day, where again the wind on that day will determine the direction up to 21st March. Having said that the main four quarter winds are 100% reliable.

If the grass is growing on 1st January (as in 2016 when it was very mild indeed), then there will be a poor hay harvest – as was proven later in the year to be the case, it was both a very late and poor hay harvest.

Certain days will determine how far behind or how far ahead the season is. Snowdrops will flower normally about 1st February, if they flower before then, then the season is mild and advanced. Crocuses will flower 14th February – St Valentine's day, again they will determine how warmer or colder the season is against the norm.

The second Sunday in May is known as 'Chestnut Sunday,' The flowers of the horse chestnut tree (conker tree) are called candles, and on the Chestnut Sunday, all these candles will stand upright at the end of each branch, and, when viewed from a distance will look just like a Christmas Tree with candles on it, all sticking bolt upright, a truly magnificent sight, and, to compliment this, nature in its infinite wisdom, guarantees a dry sunny calm day to display such a beautiful sight in all its glory. So it would be a good day for a spring wedding.

Wimbledon tennis fortnight is often beset with a rainy interlude, and there is a simple reason for this. The period 29th June to the 5th July is a Buchan Cool period, when the average temperature is lower than average, cold air therefore combines with warm air and produces rain; a hence wet interlude for the tennis.

The first Friday in July is always wet – it ALWAYS rains on the first Friday in July.

The 14th July (Bastille Day in France) is a Buchan warm day, and is accepted as one of the consistently hottest days of the UK year, a most reliable day for hot dry sunny events.

The period 13th to 15th August is also a Buchan warm period and this consistently produces a hot spell during these days.

October 18th (St Luke) starts a short period of 5 days or so, fine dry calm sunny days, between the 18th and 28th October – instantly recognisable as school half-term time, though the nights may well be cold and frosty. This is the true Indian Summer period, which mistakenly is often quoted as being in September. This period ends on the 28th (St Jude and St James) when there is ALWAYS a storm, a 100% certainty.

Christmas Day provides the best forward indicator of the year. If the sun shines on this day then a good fruit harvest and a good grain harvest are guaranteed. A massive claim but 100% correct. Christmas Day 2013 and 2014 were both dry bright and sunny, both years gave excellent fruit and grain harvests. 2016 was a wet stormy day and produced a poor fruit and grain harvest. Such sun also tells of no damaging frosts to destroy the fruit blossoms in May, and also good growing conditions and summer sun for both harvests, therefore good summer in July and August. A sure 100% bet.

If the ground is frozen and cold on 1st January then only one hay harvest in the year, so that indicates a good June since that is hay harvest time – and that after that the weather will not be conducive to a second hay harvest, be it too wet or too dry.

To forecast a drought later in the year, an excellent 100% reliable method comes in February and March – and it really accurate too. You need to have the average rainfall from the last 18 days of February to the first 10 days of March. Here in Kent it is 100mms. Measure this rainfall and compare the result to the average. However above or below the average it is will determine whether it will wetter or drier than normal – and also if a drought is possible or probable. The measurement for 2016 here was 66mm, therefore a water shortage lay ahead, but when? This now requires the knowledge of the moon phases in June, July and August to see when such a period may well occur.

In 2016, the moons showed that the last two weeks in July were both dry, hot and sunny and also the first 10 days of August at least. Therefore it was easy to indicate that such a drought was likely in July at least, and also a strong probability of a second such drought in August too. Therefore a combination of two different but quite complimentary pieces of data when used skilfully indeed produced such a perfect result.

Two full moons in the month, rare, but about every four years or so, the second full moon is called a 'Blue Moon,' hence the saying 'Once in a blue moon;' such moons too, in August will devastate the vine crop since they will bring much rain too.

As the reader goes through each monthly data sheet, there are many such occurrences that appear, but not all as certain as the above, all have their merits.

The advice is to never guess, if uncertain say so, it is better to appear ignorant than give a completely incorrect prediction. This is not a precise skill, in the UK we do not have a climate, we have weather, sometimes four seasons in a day; and as such forecasting is difficult at best. To be able to predict at least 3 months ahead takes years of skill, application, knowledge and expertise, I am not perfect, I aim for 90% accuracy. If I get it wrong, then I enquire why and admit the mistake, for it is always the human factor that goes wrong – a wrong interpretation or some small missed item of vital data – but then, none of us is perfect.

'The difficult I do straight away, the impossible takes a little longer' – to paraphrase a famous slogan.

Complete Monthly Data Sheets with all Necessary and Relevant Detail January to December Inclusive

JANUARY

NEW MOON 10th @ 01.31hrs = FROST

1st QUARTER MOON = 16th @ 23.27hrs = FAIR AND FROSTY

FULL MOON 24th @ 0146 = FROST

LAST QUARTER MOON 2nd @ 0531hrs = RAIN

DOP = 25th ST PAUL

HIGHEST SPRING TIDES 11th TO 15th

1st   Calends
        If Janiver Calends be summerly gay, wintery
        weather will continue to the Calends of May.
2nd   Apogee 1154 hrs
3rd   It will be the same weather for 9 weeks as it is the
        ninth day after Christmas.
5th   Twelfth night.
6th   Epiphany
        The days are lengthened a cocks stride.
8th   Weather before noon foretells June, weather after
        noon that of May.
9th   Weather before noon foretells August, weather after
        noon that of July.
10th   Weather before noon foretells October, weather after
        noon that of September.
11th   Plough Monday
        Weather before noon foretells that of December,
        weather afternoon that of November.
12th   If the sun shines today it foretells much wind.
13th   St Hilary
        Foretells the weather for the whole year – often
        considered the coldest and/or the wettest day of the
        year (reliable). Homage day to the apple tree.
15th   St Paul the Hermit
        If rain or snow this day there will be a blessing on
        the year.
        Perigee 0211hrs
17th   St Sulphicius
        Frost augers well for the spring.
19th – 31st
        See rhyme below.

22nd St Vincent
If the sky is clear, more water than wine will crown the year. If the sun shines today (it foreshadows much wind), prosperous weather all year.

25th St Paul aka as St Annanias
It is said to predict the weather for the whole year ahead (it is good for 6 months – but tails off after that – Ed)
DAY OF PREDICTION
Also known as Egyptian Day. Burns Night.
Arguably the most important day of the year.

30th Apogee 0911hrs

31st Hazel Tree in flower

Met Office notes
5th to 17th Stormy.
18th to 24th Quiet.
25th to 31st Stormy again.

Buchan notes
None.

Tree of the month is the BIRCH up to the 16th, thereafter the ROWAN.

General notes and comments

- As days lengthen so cold strengthens. The blackest month of the year.

- In winter, after the prevalence of easterly winds, if the barometer begins to fall and the thermometer to rise, a gale which starts to blow from the SE will veer to the SW, whilst the barometer falls constantly.

- As soon as the wind passes the SW point the barometer begins to rise, a heavy shower of rain falls, and a strong W/NW or NE wind may follow, after which, the sky clears and the weather becomes colder. [This is an exact UK weather pattern and true]

- A January spring is worth nothing.

- If no snow before the end of January there will be more in March and April.

- 1st – If this be a Sunday, winter will be cold and moist, spring windy, the summer hot, and, at harvest time wind and rain with abundance of corn and other grain.

- If this be a Monday, severe and confused winter, good spring and windy summer.

- If this be a Tuesday, dreary and severe winter. windy spring, rainy summer.

- If this a Wednesday, hard winter, bad spring, good summer.

- If this be a Thursday, good winter, windy spring, good summer.

- If this be a Friday, variable winter, good spring and summer.
- If this be a Saturday, snowy winter, blowing spring, wet summer.
- Summerish January gives winterish spring.
- January commits the fault and May bears the blame.
- If January the sun appear, March and April will pay full dear.
- When Oak trees bend with snow in January, good crops may be expected.
- March in January, January in March.
- If grass do grow in Janiveer,'twill grow the worse for all the year.
- If grain grows in January, a year of great need.
- If birds begin to whistle, frosts to come.
- Dry January plenty of wine. Wet January no wine.
- Fog in January brings a wet spring.
- Hoar frost and no snow is hurtful to fields, trees and grain.
- Wet January, wet spring.
- If January is wet the barrels stay empty (wine).
- January freeze, the pot on the fire.
- Gale force winds are quite common in January.
- Remember on St Vincent's Day (22nd), if the sun his beams display, 'Tis a token bright and clear, of prosperous weather through-out the year,
- More wine than water, much rye and wine.

- St Vincent's is normally a good weather day.

- If the birds start singing on St Vincent's day 'twill be an early spring.

- St Paul's day is also St Annanias's day (25th).

- If the sun shines on St Paul's Day it betokens a good year; if snow or rain an indifferent year. (A bad crop of grain) If cloudy and misty a great dearth and beasts and birds will die, if Thunder great winds are predicted and unrest will vex us all and cold will blow the great winds of January.

- Clouds on St Annanias Day portend floods.

- St Paul's Day – It is necessary to observe and note down the phases of the day, hour by hour, or, even half an hourly, throughout the day from 6am to 6pm. This is due to the belief that the hours of the day will reflect the weather, month by month throughout the year.

- Generally these signs are dependable up to the end of July. However there is much truth in the above and 90% accuracy is quite normal – with 100% one year.

- Snow usually falls in the third week of January. If it doesn't fall then, then it won't fall at all.

- For farmers it is wise to plan your hay crop now. If the grass is already starting to grow, then do not look for two hay crops this year for the worse it will be later on.

- The first three days of January rule the coming first three months.

- Warm January, cold May.

- There will certainly be at least one very cold snap, very likely with snow too. It has been known to arrive as early as Boxing Day (26th December) and as late as the 30th January. It will come and will probably be the worst cold snap of the year. There is much truth in the saying that the hardest winters are those that start around twelfth night (6th), following a dry December. On snow – it is generally unknown, that if snow lies for three days it will require another fall to take it away.

- If late October and early November be warm and rainy, then January and February shall be frosty and cold. [check readings from previous year]

- When the months of July, August and September are exceptionally hot, January will be the coldest month. [check previous readings]

- Windy October – dry January [check previous readings]

- A dry and frosty Janiveer is like to make a plenteous year – a very dependable saying.

- 19th–31st. These last twelve days of the month rule the weather for the whole year.

Full moon this month is known as WOLF MOON.

The tree of the month up to the 15th is BIRCH. Thereafter the ROWAN.

Monthly averages for
Edenbridge (using 1981–2010 figures)

Mean Max:	7.8C
Mean Min:	1.C
Mean Avg:	4.4C
Rainfall:	83.6mm
Sunshine:	69.3hrs (day = 2.23hrs)

The following figures are for the average temperature at 12 noon and again at 4pm, taken at the beginning and again at the end of the month.

	12 noon	4pm
1st	5.8C	5.8C
31st	5.7C	5.1C

FEBRUARY

NEW MOON = 8th @ 14.40hrs = FAIR AND MILD

1ST QUARTER MOON = 15th @ 07.47hrs = STORMY

FULL MOON 22ND @ 18.22hrs = FAIR AND FROSTY

LAST QUARTER MOON 1st @ 23.12hrs = FAIR AND FROSTY

DOP = 2nd = CANDLEMASS

HIGHEST SPRING TIDES 8th TO 14th

1st St Brigid
     If white every ditch full.
2nd Candlemass aka as Purification Day of BVM. Day
     of Prediction. Cold weather at Candlemass means
     colder weather after the feast than before.
     Snow drop blossom day.
6th St Dorothea
     Gives most snow. Apogee 06.27hrs.
12th St Eulalies
     If sun today, then good for apples and cider.
12th–14th see below.
14th St Valentine
     Crocus blossom time.
17th Shrove Tuesday
     So as the sun shines on Pancake Tuesday, the like
     will shine every day in Lent. Thunder on Shrove
     Tuesday foretelleth wind, store of fruit and plenty.
     When the sun is shining on Shrovetide day it is
     meant well for peas and rye
18th Ash Wednesday
     Where the wind lies today it will remain for all Lent.
     A dry Lent spells a fertile year.
19th Perigee 07.31hrs.
22nd St Peter
     If cold will last longer – the night gives 40 days
     weather.
     1st Sunday in Lent
24th St Mathias
     St Mattee send sap up tree (usually indicates an
     early spring). If freezing today so for a month.

28th   St Romanus
        Bright and clear indicates a good year.

Met Office notes

24th to 28th stormy.

Buchan notes

7th to 14th cold period.

General Notes and Comments

* Shortest and worst of all months.

* If Candlemass Day be clear and bright, winter will have another flight.

* But if it be dark with clouds and rain, winter has gone and will not come again.

* If Candlemass be mild and gay, go saddle your horse and buy them hay as half the winter's to come this year.

* This day is a very reliable day for wind up to the end of May. This Quarter Day is not however a true 90 day span as are the other three such Quarter days. Therefore as a Quarter Day it requires more caution.

* Where-ever the wind on Candlemass Day, there 'twill stay to the end of May.

* A snow cover in February protects the land from the worst excesses of frost and snow, and a slow thaw gently releases the water into the ground. A sudden thaw

accompanied by heavy rain is one of the most damaging of weather combinations. [causing at times severe flooding]

- February always brings the rain and thaws the frozen lakes again.

- Much February snow, April summer doth show. [yes 4/5 times true]

- A month with snow means spring will be fine.

- If freezing on the 24th – will continue for a month, St Mathias breaks the ice, if none, he breaks it.

- A sunny February brings wet and stormy summer.

- February fill dyke, be it black or be it white, but if it be white, 'tis better to like.

- [regardless of snow or rain, the ditches will usually fill during February.]

- In February if thou hearest thunder, thou shalt see a summer wonder.

- Dry February, dry summer.

- A warm day in February is a dream of summer.

- February spring ain't worth a pin.

- On Candlemass Day if thorns be a-drop you can be sure of a good pea crop. [peas are picked in June which implies a good period]

- When drops hang on the fence at Candlemass, icicles will hang on 25th March.

- When the wind's in the east, it will stay to the 2nd of May.

- If a storm then spring is near, but if bright and clear then spring is late.

- If Candlemass Day do bluster and blow, winter is over, as all do know.

- All the months of the year curse a fair Februair.

- If February brings no rain, 'tis neither good for grass or grain.

- February makes a bridge (of ice) and March breaks it.

- As the days lengthen so the cold strengthens.

- Warm February gives light hay crop, cold February gives heavy hay crop.

- Snow in February puts wheat in the granary.

- February snow burns the corn.

- If the last 18 days of February are wet and the first 10 days of March are mainly rainy, then spring quarter and summer too, will prove wet too. If dry then watch out for drought conditions in the summer.

and …

- From local figures of the above February and march dates if the combined rainfall is less than 100mms, then the drought possibility is much higher, A refined calculation. There will be a deficiency of rain up to Midsummer day.

- Fogs in February means frosts in May.

- There will be as many frosts in June as fogs in February.

- February is a damp month, not because of high rainfall, but because of low evaporation rate.

- Often a month of intense cold, as the thermometer falls and the crimson sun sits in an open sky.

- A time of burst pipes, and, in a good year, of skating.

- So, if you are to have a good summer, alas, February will need to be a cold wet miserable month.

- See reference to St Catherine – 25th November.

- At St Catherine, foul or fair, so 'twill be next Februair.

- When hottest in June – coldest in the following February. [check June readings]

- In August, so next February. [check August readings – but what relevance?]

- Warm October – cold February. [check readings]

- If late October and early November be warm and rainy, then January and February will be frosty and cold. [check previous readings.]

- With every thunder with rain in February, there will be a cold spell in May.

- Isolated fine days in February are considered as certain to be followed by a storm.

- A dry Lent spells a fertile year.

The full moon this month is known as the SNOW MOON.

ROWAN is the tree of the month up to 17th. Then ASH takes over.

Monthly averages for
Edenbridge (using 1981–2010 figures)

Mean Max:	8.7C
Mean Min:	0.2C
Mean Avg:	4.45C
Rainfall:	54.1mm
Sunshine:	87.9hrs (day = 3.14hrs)

The following figures are for the average temperature at 12 noon and again at 4pm, taken at the beginning and again at the end of the month.

	12 noon	4pm
1st	5.7C	5.2C
31st	7.6C	8.8C

MARCH

NEW MOON = 9th @ 0155hrs = FROST

1st QUARTER MOON = 15th @ 1740hrs = FAIR

FULL MOON 23rd @ 1201hrs = SNOW AND RAIN + LUNAR
ECLIPSE

LAST QUARTER MOON 1st @ 2312hrs = FAIR AND FROSTY
AND 31st @ 1618hrs = FAIR

DOP = 21st ST BENEDICT AND QUARTER DAY 21st

VERNAL EQUINOX = 20th

SOLAR ECLIPSE = 8th

LUNAR ECLIPSE = 23rd

HIGHEST SPRING TIDES 8th TO 14th

PERIGEE 10th @ 0730hrs: APOGEE 25th @ 1417hrs

1st   St David
Ever on St David's day, put oats and barley in clay.
2nd Sunday in Lent

2nd   St Chad
Every goose lays before St Chad, whether good goose or bad [if your goose has not laid by this day start fattening for the pot for she is not a good layer] Sow peas today.

3rd   St Winneral
The holy day of the saint who controls tides and weather. If stormy today bad winds to follow, but quiet end to the end of the month.

5th   Apogee 07.36hrs

6th   4th in Lent
Mothering Sunday

10th   Perigee @ 0730hrs

13th   5th in Lent
Simnel Sunday

15th   Cheltenham Races 15th to 18th

16th   St Piran
Cornish festival

17th   St Patrick
Around this time Cheltenham Gold Cup race meeting and some freakish weather.

19th   St Joseph of Nazareth
A fertile year if clear and dry.

20th   Vernal equinox.
Palm Sunday If weather not clear this day it means a bad year. If thunder today a merry year.

21st   St Benedict
DoP. Quarter Day. As the wind today it will stay for
three months.
A fertile day if not freezing today. See below for
frost precautions.

24th   Maundy Thursday Fine on Holy Thursday, wet on
Whit Monday (25th May).

25th   Lady Day
Virgin Mary Day, The day the cardamine flower
blooms. Daffodil blossom day. Apogee @ 1417hrs.
Good Friday
DoP up to 25th May (St Urban). Rain on Good
Friday and Easter Day, good year for grass and a bad
one for hay (wet June). – This signifies a wet year
and such weather on Good Friday will last for 40
days.

27th   Easter Day
If sunshine today, so at Whitsun (24th May). Rainy
Easter = cheesy year (wet). Greenfly at Easter – June
will blister.

BST Starts.

Met Office notes
None.

Buchan notes
None.

General Notes and Comments.

- The Four wind days, Quarter Days, are among the most reliable in the year and give the prevailing wind until the next Quarter Day.

- The month of renewal – The month of winds and new life. March – many weathers.

- If the winds for Candlemass (2nd February) and St Benedict (21st) are contradictory, then St Benedict takes preference.

- 10th – If it does not freeze, a fertile year may be expected; mists or hoar frosts indicate a plentiful year, but not without some diseases.

- 21st, St Benedict. This Quarter Day will give you the wind up to 24th June (St John)

- which is just 95 days later. St Benedict will take precedence over Candlemass should the winds directions be contradictory.

- St Benedict – sow thy peas or keep them in the nick.

- March is traditionally a boisterous month throughout the temperate zones of the northern hemisphere. The reason is that the polar regions are at their coldest after nearly six months of night, while the equatorial regions are at their hottest because the sun is overhead.

- The strength of the atmospheric circulation depends primarily on the difference of temperature between the equator and poles; hence it is most vigorous when the contrasts of hot and cold are greatest in March.

- When there has been no particular storm about the time of the spring equinox, if a storm arise from the east on or before that day, or, if a storm from any point of the compass arise a week after the equinox, then, in either of these cases, the succeeding summer is generally dry (4/5). But if a storm arise from the SW or WSW or a frost before the spring equinox, the summer is generally wet. (5/6).

- There are generally some warm days at the end of March or the beginning of April, which will bring the Blackthorn into bloom, and, which are followed by a cold period called the Blackthorn Winter (11–14th April). Fogs in March – frosts in May. [This is quite accurate, in London there are on average four foggy mornings in March and four nights average ground frost in May]

- Fog in March – Thunder in July. [doubtful].

- As much fog in March, so much rain in summer.

- As it rains in March so in June. [doubtful]

- A wet March makes a sad harvest.

- March damp and warm does the farmer much harm.

- When March has April weather, April will have March weather.

- Dry March, wet April, dry May and wet June are generally said to bring everything in tune.

- A windy March and a rainy April makes a beautiful May.

- A showery March and a showery May portend a wholesome summer – if there be a showery April between.

- Dust in March brings grass and foliage.
- A peck of March dust to be sold, is worth a King's ransom.
- March dust on apple leaf, brings all kinds of fruit to grief.
- The March sun rises but dissolves not. March sun lets snow stand on a stone.
- If you've March in January then January will appear in March
- After a frosty winter there will be a good fruit harvest.
- If March winds start early it will be a dry Easter.
- A dry lent spells a fertile year.
- A windy/dry March fortells a dry May.
- March flowers make no summer bowers.
- March dry – good rye.
- A dry cold March never begs its bread.[a good grain harvest implies a dry July and August]
- March snow hurts the seeds.
- Snow in March is bad for fruit and grape vines.
- Moles are a good guide for a fortnight or so, it is a sure sign of warmer weather when they start to become active – it may only be a short warm period.
- Field mice however, when scurrying around are a prelude to bad weather. They are laying in stocks of food.
- Better bitten by a snake than feel the sun in March.

- March, month of many weathers, wildly comes in hail and snow and threatening floods and burns.
- A peck of March dust and a shower in May makes the corn green and meadows all gay.
- The month of winds and new life.
- After a frosty winter there will be a good pea harvest.
- For the elderly – February search, March try – April says whether you live or die.
- Average central England temperature is 5.7C.
- Broadly speaking, significant plant growth commences at 6C or above.
- Winter = –6C. Summer = +6C.
- March tends to be the driest month of the year – but subject to cold snaps and frost.
- The third week of March is often the driest of the whole year.
- It is also said that March borrows its last week from April, which indicates the tail of the month is often more spring like than the rest of it.
- The last three days are called 'borrowing days' for if they are unusually stormy, March is said to have borrowed them from April. Three days of wind and rain is more the norm.
- Also – one day rain. one day snow and the other, the worst day they ever knew.
- The third week of the month (around the 17th St Patrick's day) is fronted by Cheltenham Gold Cup race meeting. This period will certainly produce a

combination of most variable weather, from rain/snow/sleet and winds to hot dry and sunny.

- March is usually a very varied month and a sensible traveller will be prepared for anything.

- If March comes in like a lion it will go out like a lamb (and vice-versa). [dependable, but it only applies to the first and last two or three days of the month]

- If March comes in all stormy and black, she carries winter away on her back.

- As in September, so next March – sometimes. [check previous September readings]

- As in October wet, March dry: yes if October wet is above average then March below average. October cold, March (warm) cold – is more likely cold from local records.

- October warm, March colder than average – from local records.

- If the last 18 days of February are wet and the first 10 days of March be for the most part rainy, then the spring and summer quarters are likely to be wet too, and a drought is unknown but that it entered that season. [this is very true – so watch the drought situation]

and…

- If the rainfall from the above dates is less than 100mms then the drought possibility is far higher. This is a refined local calculation.

- Northerly winds over northern Europe reach their highest frequency around 15th June. But are rare after 20th June. Meanwhile SW winds blow comparatively infrequently from late March until 10th June, but are very much more common during the rest of June.

- From the same research, taking England and Wales as a whole, the driest months of the year are: March, April and May, and occasionally February and June. These months are also the months when long drags of unsettled westerly winds are unlikely to occur. Monthly rainfall is between 2.3/2.6 ins (58/66mms) for each month from February to June.

- From July onwards 3.2/3.8ins (81/96mms).

- A dry Lent spells a fertile year.

Full moon this month is known as the SAP MOON.

The tree of the month up to the 17th is the ASH. Thereafter the ALDER.

Monthly averages for
Edenbridge (using 1981–2010 figures)

Mean Max:	12.1C
Mean Min:	2.4C
Mean Avg:	7.25C
Rainfall:	56.2mm
Sunshine:	142.2hrs (day = 4.58hrs)

The following figures are for the average temperature at 12 noon and again at 4pm, taken at the beginning and again at the end of the month.

	12 noon	4pm
1st	7.1C	7C
31st	12.4C	13.1C

APRIL

NEW MOON = 7th @ 1225hrs = SNOW/RAIN

1ST QUARTER MOON = 14th @ 0500hrs = STORMY

FULL MOON 22nd @ 0625hrs = STORMY

LAST QUARTER MOON 30th @ 04.30hrs = RAIN

HIGHEST SPRING TIDES 7th TO 11th

APOGEE 21st @ 1606hrs: PERIGEE 7th @ 1737hrs

BUCHAN COLD PERIOD 11th – 14th

1st   All Fools Day. Should it rain on All Fools Day, it brings good crops of corn and hay.

3rd   Low Sunday This Sunday settles the weather for the whole summer

4th   Hop Monday   Hop pole erection day.

6th   Latter Lady Day – the cold comes on the water.

7th   Perigee @ 1737hrs

10th   Pastor Sunday If it rains this day it will rain every Sunday until Pentecost (15th May).

11th–14th
        Blackthorn Winter

14th   Cuckoo Day
        The cuckoos song is first heard about this time.

15th   St Basilissa
        Swallows arrive.

16th   St Padarn
        Celtic Goddess – traditionally the day to start weeding growing crops.

21st   Apogee @ 1606hrs

23rd   St George
        Comes the cuckoo and the nightingale. When St George growls (thunder) in the sky, wind and storms are drawing nigh.
        Harebell flowering day.
        Mallard Day – From a festival at All Souls College, Oxford. Perigee 0024hrs

23rd to 26th
        A cold stormy period bringing heavy showers.

25th   St Mark As long before this day frogs are heard a-croaking, so long will they keep quiet afterwards.

The cuckoo heralds the arrival of migratory birds from the south, indicating the return of summer.

Met Office notes

None.

Buchan notes

11th to 14th is cold period.

General Notes and Comments

- The month of seasonal changes, young leaves and blossoms unfold. April and May are the keys to the whole year.
- The first really cheerful month of the year.
- Rarely a very wet month, can be completely dry.
- Annual humidity is at its lowest and can produce dust storms.
- Hottest ever April in 2007/2011
- As a general rule, April weather is a mixture of all sorts.
- April weather, rain and sunshine together.
- We must suffer a cold wet April if we want a good summer.
- Cold weather in April is supposed to be good for bumper harvest. A cold April – barn will fill.
- A dry March and a rainy April makes a beautiful May.

- Most old sayings say it is best to have a wet April.
- When April blows his horn, 'tis good for hay and corn. [the reference to 'horn' means thunder, it also means a good summer]
- April cold and wet fills the barns best yet.
- April wet, good wheat.
- After a cold April the barns fill best.
- April cold and wet fills barns and barrels.
- April rain makes large sheaves.
- April showers bring May flowers.
- East wind in spring a brilliant summer will bring.
- When doves start to coo the last frosts have gone.
- After a wet April a dry June. After a moist April a clear June.
- Spring has come when a virgin can cover six daisies with her foot.
- When winter meets summer it fortells a hot dry summer [sometimes a prolonged winter seems to turn into summer overnight].
- The weather in the second half of April fortells the summer. [wise words commanding respect]
- Cloudy April – dewy May. Thunderstorms in April – floods in May.
- Showery April – Flowery May.
- Dry Spring – wet Autumn. Thunder in spring and cold it will bring.
- Blackthorn Winter – 11th–14th April.

- Just as the Blackthorn is coming into blossom expect some fine weather. However if the flower arrives before the leaf then expect a cold snap.

and …

- If he blooms before the leaves appear, be sure there will be a bitter spell – perhaps even with snow. [this is a most accurate saying]
- 23rd St Georges Day – If it rains today St George eats all the cherries.
- Much February snow – April summer doth show. [check records]
- Early Cuckoo – dry summer (arrival in or before early April). The later he arrives the worse the summer.
- When March has April weather, April will have March weather.
- E/NE winds reach their greatest frequency during April and May.
- After a warm April and a warm October, a warm year to come.
- A dry Lent spells a fertile year.
- April, more than March, can have both summer and winter embrace it. April can also be more snowy than December. Classic April snowstorms of 1966 &1981. Whilst in 1949 the mercury topped 80F(27C).
- April has the face of a monk and the claws of a cat.
- Thunderstorms in April is the end of hoar-frost.

- If the first three days be foggy, there will be a flood in June. (rain in June will make the lanes boggy)

- April may be famous for its showers, but it is rarely a very wet month. Quite the contrary – April is one of the driest months of the year in all parts of the UK.

- Greenfly at Easter, June will blister.

- Rainy Easter – a cheesy year (much rain = plenty of grass)

- Northerly winds over northern Europe reach their highest frequency around 15th June; But are rare after 20th June. Meanwhile SW winds blow comparatively infrequently from late March until 10th June, but are very much more common during the rest of June.

- From the same research, taking England and Wales as a whole, the driest months of the year are: – March, April and May, and occasionally February and June. These months are also the months when long drags of unsettled westerly winds are unlikely to occur. Monthly rainfall is between 2.3/2.6 inches (58/66mms) for each month from February to June.

- From July onwards 3.2/3.8ins (81/96mms).

- 23rd/26th – A cold stormy period brings heavy showers.

- There is also a similar period mid-month.

- Tidal energies are ruled by moon particularly this month, possibly the reason for the severely changeable weather at this time.

The full moon this month is known as the PINK MOON.

The tree of the month up to the 14th is the ALDER. Thereafter is the WILLOW.

Monthly averages for
Edenbridge (using 1981–2010 figures)

Mean Max:	15.5C
Mean Min:	3.3C
Mean Avg:	9.4C
Rainfall:	60.5mm
Sunshine:	191.9hrs (day = 6.4hrs)

The following figures are for the average temperature at 12 noon and again at 4pm, taken at the beginning and again at the end of the month.

	12 noon	4pm
1st	12.2C	5.8C
31st	14.4C	15.5C

MAY

NEW MOON = 6th @ 2031hrs = RAINY

1ST QUARTER MOON = 13th @ 1803hrs = FAIR

FULL MOON 21st @ 2216hrs = FAIR

LAST QUARTER MOON 29th @ 1313hrs = CHANGEABLE

DOP = 25th ST URBAN

HIGHEST SPRING TIDES 5th TO 10th

APOGEE 18th @ 2207hrs: PERIGEE 6th @ 0415hrs

BUCHAN COLD PERIOD 9th – 14th

1st   May Day

Hoar frost today indicates good harvest. Plants in full growth.

The later the Blackthorn blooms after 1st May, the better the rye.

3rd   Holy Cross Day

Crowfoot blossom time.

St Philip and St James

If it rains, a fertile year may be expected, and it foretells a wet harvest.

5th   Ascension Day

As the weather today so may be the entire autumn

6th   Perigee @ 0415hrs

10th   Chestnut Sunday

11th   St Mamertus

Ice-Saint – beware of frost – unseasonally cold and/ or wet weather}

12th   St Pancras

.........as 11th ....Ice Maidens = night frost}

13th   St Servatius

.........as 11th ....}

14th   St Boniface

.........as 11th ....}

15th   Pentecost

If sun shines Easter Day (20th April) so it will at Whitsun. Strawberries at Whitsuntide = good wine. If it happens to rain on Whitsunday, thunder and lightning would follow (Thunder yes, but much rain is doubtful). Rain at Whitsunday is said make the wheat mildew. Whitsun wet = Christmas fat. Whitsun rain is a blessing on the wine.

16th   Whit Monday The weather today reflects that of
        Maundy Thursday (24th March)
18th   Apogee @ 2207hrs
19th   St Dunstan (cold Sophie). Ice Saint with
        characteristics as above for ice-maidens.
22nd   Dandelion picking day in East Anglia for dandelion
        wine. Trinity Sunday
24th   Celtic celebration day for bringing prosperity and
        good harvest.
25th   St Urban
        DoP. Day of Prediction up to 15th June (St Vitus).
        Summer starts.
26th   Corpus Christi
        Clear gives a good year. If rain, the granary will be
        light.

Met Office notes
None.

Buchan notes
9th to 14th cold period.

General notes and comments.

* If you are looking for a good summer, the best May
  weather you need should be cold and rainy.
* May can be/likely to be cold, but nothing strange in this.

- He who dofts his coat on a winter's day will gladly put it on in May.

- A cold May gives full barns and empty churchyards.

- Goddess of Spring. Sacred Hawthorn tree blossoms this month.

- Severe gales are very much the exception to the rule, though boisterous breezes are fairly common.

- E/NE winds reach their greatest frequency during April and May.

- SE England, London in particular, suffers from more short intense storms than any other part of the country.

- April and May are the best time to visit Scotland.

- The later the Blackthorn in bloom after the 1st May, the better the rye and harvest.

- He who shears his sheep before St Mamertus Day (11th) loves his wool more than his sheep.

- If rough winds do shake the darling buds of May, and summer's lease hath all too short a stay.

- A cold wet May is good for corn and hay, a dry May fortells a wholesome summer.

- Flowers in May good cocks of hay. Water in May – bread all year.

- Rain in May makes plenty of hay.

- A cold May and windy, a full barn will find ye.

- St Urban (25th) gives the summer.

- Ne're cast a clout till May be out, button to chin till June be in, if you change in June you change too soon.

- Change in July? You'll catch a cold bye and bye.
- Change in August if you must.
- Be sure to remember change back in September.
- Mist in May, heat in June, puts the harvest right in tune/ makes the harvest come right soon.
- A leaky May and dry June makes harvest come right soon.
- A May flood never did anyone any good.
- Who sows his oats in May has little to repay.
- A swarm of bees in May is worth a load of hay.
- When bees leave their hive then it's good to be alive, when they all go home again then it's surely going to rain.
- When the Mulberry tress begins to shoot, the last frost has gone. [Impeccable reference]
- Spring will not settle properly until the cowslips have died down.
- When September has been rainy, the following May is generally dry; and when May is dry, September is apt to be wet. [check previous readings in each case]
- [the above however is not really reliable – however – If May is well above the average for rain then the same can be said for September being above average for rain too.

and…

- If May is drier than average then September is likely to be drier than average too.
- ALL THE ABOVE FROM LOCAL READINGS.
- Fogs in March – frosts in May.

- [this is quite accurate. In London there on average, four foggy mornings in March and an average of four nights of ground frost in May. Check local readings]

- Franklins Frost strikes Devon 19th, 20th and 21st May.

- To conclude. May is a most uncertain month. A month of variable temperatures and rainfall.

- Northerly winds over northern Europe reach their highest frequency around 15th June. But are rare after 20th June.

- Meanwhile SW winds blow comparatively infrequently from late March until 10th June, but are very much more common during the rest of June.

- From the same research, taking England and Wales as a whole, the driest months of the year are: March, April and May, and occasionally February and June. These months are also the months when long drags of unsettled westerly winds are unlikely to occur.

- Monthly rainfall is between 2.3/2.6 ins (58/66mms) for each month from February to June.

- From July onwards 3.2/3.8ins (81/96mms).

- The hay crop is harvested at the end of May and June, so any reference to a good hay crop implies good weather then.

- A hot May makes a fat churchyard.

- A May wet was never kind yet, a May flood never did good.

- Mud in May, grain in August.

- Cool and evening due in May, brings wine and much hay.

- The more thunder in May, the less in August and September.

The full moon this month known as FLOWER MOON.

The tree of the month up to 12th is the WILLOW. Thereafter HAWTHORN from 13th.

Monthly averages for
Edenbridge (using 1981–2010 figures)

Mean Max	19.3C
Mean Min:	7.1C
Mean Avg:	13.2C
Rainfall:	58.9mm
Sunshine:	197.8hrs (Day = 6.38hrs)

The following figures are for the average temperature at 12 noon and again at 4pm, taken at the beginning and again at the end of the month.

	12 noon	4pm
1st	15.7C	16.9C
31st	18.8C	19.9C

JUNE

NEW MOON = 5th @ 2031hrs = RAINY

1ST QUARTER MOON = 12th @ 0910hrs = FREQUENT
SHOWERS

FULL MOON 20th @ 1204hrs = VERY RAINY

LAST QUARTER MOON 27th @ 1920hrs = RAINY

DOP = 15th ST VITUS AND 24th ST JOHN

HIGHEST SPRING TIDES = 4th TO 8th

APOGEE 15th @ 1201hrs: PERIGEE 3rd @ 1056hrs

BUCHAN COLD PERIOD 26th TO 4th JULY

3rd   Perigee @1056hrs

8th   St Medard
        Rain today and it tells of a wet harvest. If rain today,
        rain 40 days after(18/7)

11th   St Barnabas
        Nearly always a clear fine day, a noteworthy day
        too. Rain today good for grapes. Ragged Robin
        flowering time.

15th   St Vitus
        DoP. See rain note below. Apogee @ 1201hrs

19th   St Protais
        If the saint brings rain 40 days it will remain.
        Father's day.

20th   Summer Solstice 2234hrs.

24th   St JohnDoP. Midsummer. Longest Day. Quarter
        Day. Rain today and expect a wet harvest and
        damage to nuts. Scarlet Lynchis flowering
        day. Midsummer rain spoils hay and grain.

27th   If rain today then rain for 7 weeks.

29th   St Peter and St Paul
        Rain will rot the roots of rye. The optimal day for
        harvesting herbs.

Met Office notes

None.

Buchan notes

29th June to 4th July cold period.

General Notes and comments.

- The month needs to be 'flaming' for a good harvest.
- If June with bright sun is blessed, for harvest we will thank the Goddess.
- SW winds are generally infrequent before 10th June, after that they are quite frequent.
- The month of the return of the 'westerly winds.'
- The month of June is blithe and gay, driving winter's ills away.
- Calm weather in June sets the corn in tune.
- It can be a very hot month (1976 and 1996, 2003, 2006 and 2012) and very wet (1997 and 2007).
- When it is hottest in June it will be coldest in the following February.
- When the wind shifts to the west in early June expect wet weather until the end of August.
- In June, the Cuckoo changes his tune from 'cuckoo' to 'cuck-cuckoo', sometimes when you hear two preliminary 'cucks' – when this occurs a particularly fine spell is due.
- Wimbledon tennis, last week in June and first week in July.
- Barnabas (11th) bright, all day and all night.[quite reliable and really noteworthy day – always a fine clear day]
- Rain today good for grapes.

Weather notes

- St Barnabas – mow your first grass. [this applies to field grass and in the south a few days earlier]

- When Barnabas smiles bright both day and night -poor Ragged Robin (wild flower) bloom in the hay. (a great time for weed growth)

- If St Vitus Day (15th) be rainy weather, 'twill rain for thirty to forty days together. [maybe thirty days is a better ruling- and it becomes quite a reliable rule]

- As the wind on St Johns Day (24th) so 'twill be for the next three months. [until the next Quarter Day – 29th September]

- Midsummer Day (24th) rain spoils hay and grain.[a very important day as well as the longest]

- Midsummer day rain spoils hay and grain.

- You may shear your sheep when the Elder blossoms peep.

- A dripping June keeps all in tune.

- Calm weather in June, sets the corn in tune.

- Sunny June, early harvest.

- No dew indicates rain.

- A leaky June brings the harvest soon.

- A swarm of bees in June is worth a silver spoon.

- Before St Johns Day we pray for rain – afterwards we get it anyway.

- If the Cuckoo sings after St Johns Day, the harvest will be late. [always dependable]

- If Midsummer Day be ever so little rain, the Hazel and the Walnut will be scarce, and corn smitten in many places. But apples, pears and plums will not be hurt.
- Filberts (nuts) will also be spoilt.
- Cut thistles before St John or you'll have two in place of one.
- June damp and warm does the farmer no harm.
- THE NEXT THREE ARE INFALLIBLE.
- Good summer brings hard winter.
- If a hard winter is followed by a poor summer, the following winter will be harder still.
- If the Cuckoo delays changing his tune until mid-June, St Swithuns Day (15th July) will be wet.
- June is a wet month with usually more wet days than any other month.
- Wet June – dry September.
- As it rains in March – so in June. [check previous readings]
- In Hay season when there is no dew, it indicates rain.
- If north wind blows in June, good rye harvest.
- Rain at Whitsuntide is said to make wheat mildew.
- Whitsuntide rain is a blessing for wine.
- Whitsuntide wet, Christmas fat.
- Northerly winds over northern Europe reach their highest frequency around 15th June. But are rare after 20th June. Meanwhile SW winds blow comparatively infrequently from late March until 10th June, but are very much more common during the rest of June.

- From the same research, taking England and Wales as a whole, the driest months of the year are: March, April and May, and occasionally February and June.

- These months are also the months when long drags of unsettled westerly winds are unlikely to occur. Monthly rainfall is between 2.3/2.6 ins (58/66mms) for each month from February to June. From July onwards 3.2/3.8ins (81/96mms).

- The hay crop is harvested at the end of May and June, so any reference to a good hay crop implies good weather then.

- If it rains on the 27th , it will rain for 7 weeks.

- A cold and wet June spoils the rest of the year.

- If it rains on the 29th (St Peter's Day) the bakers will have to carry double flour and single water; if dry they will carry single flour and double water.

- Rain on St Peter (29th) will the roots of rye.

- A north wind in June blows in a good rye harvest (hay harvest).

- When the bramble blossoms early in June, an early harvest can be expected.

The full moon this month is called a STRONG SUN MOON.

Tree of the month up to 9th is HAWTHORN. Thereafter is the OAK.

Monthly averages for
Edenbridge (using 1981–2010 figures)

Mean Max:	22.2C
Mean Min:	10C
Mean Avg:	16.1C
Rainfall:	52.5mm
Sunshine:	220.7hrs (day = 7.36hrs)

The following figures are for the average temperature at 12 noon and again at 4pm, taken at the beginning and again at the end of the month.

	12 noon	4pm
1st	18.1C	18.4C
30st	20.1C	21.7C

JULY

NEW MOON = 4th @ 1203hrs = VERY RAINY

1ST QUARTER MOON = 12th @ 05.05hrs = COLD AND SHOWERS

FULL MOON 19th @ 03.20hrs =FAIR

LAST QUARTER MOON 27th @ 0002hrs = FAIR

DOP = 15th ST SWITHUN

HIGHEST SPRING TIDES 5th TO 8th AND 22nd TO 24th

APOGEE 13th @ 0525hrs: PERIGEE 1st @ 0646hrs AND 27th @ 1126hrs

1st   If the first week of July be rainy weather -'twill rain
       more or less for a full four weeks.
       It always rains on the first Friday in July.
       Perigee @0646hrs.

2nd   St Mary
       If it rains today it will rain for 4 weeks.

3rd   St Thomas
       Rain today, rain for seven weeks. Commencement of
       Dog Days (to 28/8) hottest part of the year.

4th   St Bullion
       Start of Dog Days

4th to 16th
       If fine and summery, the rest of the summer is likely
       to be fine.

5th   Perigee 19.55hrs

10th   Celtic Knut the Reaper with hay cutting scythe
       worshipped. (hay making period).

13th   Apogee @ 0525hrs

14th   St Processus and St Martinian   If it rains today
       it suffocates the corn.
       Statistically the day with the highest average
       temperature.

15th   St Swithun
       DoP. Said to mark the weather for 40 days. Lily
       flowering day.

16th   Gather bunches of lavender to hang in wardrobes for
       perfume and to repel insects.

20th   St Margaret
       If rain, then talk of Margaret's flood – see below.
       Poppy flowering day.

22nd   St Mary Magdalene
Alluding to the wet, usually prevalent about the
middle of July, the saying is 'St Mary is washing her
handkerchief to go to her cousin's St James's, fair
(25th). Rose flowering day.

25th   St James
'Til St James be come and gone, you may have hops
and you may have none.

27th   Perigee 11.26hrs

29th –31st
Can be very hot days.

Met Office notes
None.

Buchan notes
12th –15th Warm period, 29th June to 4th July cool period.

General Notes and Comments

- The 'meadow month' or 'hay month' – traditional labour
  of month being hay-making.

- July should be, and quite often is, a month of blazing
  sunshine and soaring temperatures.

- Hay making and harvesting in full swing.

- Dog-Days – the moist sultry days in a period of 20
  days before and 20 days after the rising of the Dog-Star

Sirius. If we are to have a summer at all, this is the most likely time.

- Roughly from mid-July to the end of August, or, corn harvest time. Sirius is the brightest star in the heavens,and is one of those in the southern constellation Canis Major.

- As the Dog-days commence so they end. Bright and clear indicate a happy year, but accompanied by rain, for better times our hopes are vain.

- St Swithuns Day (15th) if thou dost rain, full forty days it will remain. [this saying never comes true]

- If on St Swithuns feast the welkin lours, and ever pent house streams with nasty showers, twice twenty days shall clouds their fleeces drain, and wash the pavements with incessant rain. [not really acceptable as continuous rain, but acceptable as showers/showery with bright intervals might be acceptable]

- St Swithun's day is normally a 'bit of both' day, half sunny and half wet. 'Sunny intervals and showers.' Despite the 40 days rain tag, it is more accurate to say 'sunny intervals and showers.'

- If it rains on St Swithuns Day. the saint is christening the apples, and they will be sweet and plentiful.

- Watch the weather from the 4th to 16th July. If it is fine and summery, the rest of summer is likely to be fine. [this is quite possibly true]

- If about St Swithun's (15th) a change of weather takes place, we likely to have a spell of fine or wet weather.

- When the sun enters Leo, the greatest heat then arise.

- In July, shear your rye.

- When the Goats-Beard (wild flower) closes its flowers before mid-day, then there is rain in the air. If it stays late with its petals open, the atmosphere is dry and the weather set fair.

- When the clover leaves are shut (even with clear sky and rising glass) and reaching for the sky, reach for your brolly. [very reliable]

- St Margaret (20th) – so much rain often falls this day that people speak of Margarets Flood.

- A shower in July when the corn begins to fill, is worth a plough of oxen, and that belongs theretill.

- Much thunder in July injures wheat and barley.

- In July cut your rye.

- What is to thrive in September must be baked in July. [grapes are a perfect example]

- When the months of July, August and September are exceptionally hot, January will be the coldest month. [can be confirmed- but not always]

- The first Friday in July is invariably wet. [4/5]

- Fog in March -Thunder in July. [check previous readings]

- A poor forecast for wheat indicates wet weather in July and August.

- A swarm of bees is not worth a fly.
The full moon this month is called BUCK MOON.

Tree of the month up-to 7th is OAK. Thereafter HOLLY is the tree.

Monthly averages for
Edenbridge (using 1981–2010 figures)

Mean Max:	24C
Mean Min:	12.1C
Mean Avg:	18.5C
Rainfall:	66.6mm
Sunshine:	220.3hrs (day = 7.11hrs)

The following figures are for the average temperature at 12 noon and again at 4pm, taken at the beginning and again at the end of the month.

	12 noon	4pm
1st	18.9C	19.5C
31st	21.9C	23.4C

AUGUST

NEW MOON = 2nd @ 2146hrs = FAIR

1ST QUARTER MOON = 10th @ 1922hrs = RAINY

FULL MOON 18th @ 1029hrs = FREQUENT SHOWERS + LUNAR ECLIPSE

LAST QUARTER MOON 25th @ 0444hrs = RAIN

DOP = 6th TRANSFIGURATION DAY(MAYBE) AND 24th ST BARTHOLOMEW

HIGHEST SPRING TIDES 19th TO 23rd

APOGEE 10th @ 0006hrs: PERIGEE 22nd @ 0122hrs

1st   Lammas (loafmass) – after Lammas the crop ripens as much by night as by day.
First grain harvest of the year. Camomile flowering day.

6th   Transfiguration Day
DoP. As the weather this day of Transfiguration, so it will be for the rest of the year. This over-ambitious at best, unreliable, out of sequence, and as far as I am concerned cannot seriously be considered as a DoP.

10th   St Lawrence
If sunshine and fine, good autumn and much wine. Virgins Bower flowering day. Apogee @ 0006hrs.

12th   St Clare

18th   Assumption Day
If sunshine, much and good wine. Lunar Eclipse. St Filbert Harvest day for cob-nuts.

22nd   Perigee @ 0122hrs

24th   St Bartholomew
DoP. 1st day of Autumn. Maybe, on experience, 5th September is a better day of prediction. Sunflower flowering day.

28th   End of Dog days.

Met Office notes
None.

Buchan notes
6th to 11th cool period.
12th to 15th warm period (can be very hot)

General Notes and Comments

- The harvest month.

- Statistically, August, in this area, is the wettest month of the year.

- If two full moons then sure to be wet

- A cold August after a warm July is said to signify the approach of a hard dry winter.

- When a hot dry August follows a hot dry July it portends an early and cold winter.

- Can also be a 'Disaster' month. Lynmouth Flooding 1952 (15–16th). Fastnet Yacht Race Storm 1979. Folkestone Flooding 1996 (12th). East Devon Floods 1997 (8th).

- Boscastle Flooding (2004)17th.

- Quite cold and sunless 2007

- Dog-Days – the moist sultry days in a period of 20 days before and 20 days after the rising of the Dog-Star Sirius. If we are to have a summer at all, this is the most likely time.

- Roughly from mid-July to the end of August, or, corn harvest time. Sirius is the brightest star in the heavens, and is one of those in the southern constellation Canis Major.

- As the Dog-days commence so they end. Bright and clear indicate a happy year, but accompanied by rain, for better times our hopes are vain.

- Observe on what day the first heavy fog occurs, and expect a hard frost on the same day in October.

- A fog in August also indicates a severe winter and plenty of snow. [very reliable and proven]

- As August. so next February.

- So many August fogs, so many winter mists.

- The first week of August is unusually warm, the winter will be white and long. [reliable and proven]

- All the tears that St Swithun (15th July) can cry St Bartelmys (24th) mantle WILL dry up. [be warned however that this can be out by as much as +/– 3 days]

- If St Swithuns is dry.
  If Bartholomews be fine and clear, then hope for a prosperous Autumn that year. [after this day expect dull or fine weather, but not, as a rule, much rain]

- August fills the barn and September the loft.

- Dry August and warm does the farmer no harm.

- A wet rainy August makes hard bread crust.

- St Bartholomew's Day – a most important day. Brings cold dew (campers beware). The day to start collecting honey, and the day delicate flowers should be brought indoors. If the weather is settled this day, a fine Autumn is promised. If however it rains this day, then it will rain for 40 days thereafter (to 3rd October). If misty and a morning hoar frost, the cold weather will come soon with a hard winter too.

- There is however a distinct possibility that 5th September will be a better Day of Prediction then 24th August, and, by experience is a better predicter.

- A warm dry August surely means a snowy winter.
- August thunder promises fat grapes and fine vintages. [fairly shaky for hail will damage the grapes]
- Late August, when 3 kestrels fly –'twill be dry. [reliable]
- Too much August sun disappoints the maid, the priest and the host, for it scorches up the vegetables.
- A warm Autumn is usually followed by a long winter.
- A poor forecast for wheat indicates wet weather in July and August.
- A heavy apple crop points to a fine August and September.
- When the dew is heavy in August, the weather generally remains fair. Thunderstorms in the beginning of August will generally be followed by others all the month.
- Thunderstorms after the 24th are generally violent.

The full moon for this month is called STURGEON/CORN MOON.

Tree of the month up-to 4th is HOLLY. Thereafter is HAZEL.

Monthly averages for
Edenbridge (using 1981–2010 figures)

Mean Max:	24C
Mean Min:	12.1C
Mean Avg:	18.15C
Rainfall:	66.1mm
Sunshine:	198.2hrs (day = 6.39hrs)

The following figures are for the average temperature at 12 noon and again at 4pm, taken at the beginning and again at the end of the month.

	12 noon	4pm
1st	21.8C	23.2C
31st	20.2C	21.4C

SEPTEMBER

NEW MOON = 1st @ 1004hrs = FREQUENT SHOWERS

1ST QUARTER MOON = 9th @ 1250hrs = VERY RAINY

FULL MOON 16th @ 2007hrs = RAINY + LUNAR ECLIPSE

LAST QUARTER MOON 23rd @ 10.59hrs = FREQUENT
SHOWERS

DOP = 29th ST MICHAEL (MICHAELMASS)

LUNAR ECLIPSE 16th; SOLAR ECLIPSE 1st

EQUINOX 22nd @ 2002hrs

HIGHEST SPRING TIDES 17th TO 21st

APOGEE 6th @ 1845hrs: PERIGEE 18th @ 1701hrs

DANGER WARNING: FULL MOON + PERIGEE + HIGHEST
SPRING TIDES + LUNAR ECLIPSE 16th TO 18th. EXPECT
SEVERE WEATHER PROBLEMS

1st   St Giles
        Fair on the first – fair for the month. First three
        days of the month rule the weather for October,
        November and December.

5th   Maybe this day is a better unofficial indicator than
        24th August of dryer weather.

6th   Apogee @ 1845hrs

8th   Feast of the Nativity
        As today so for the next 4 weeks.

14th   Holy Cross Day
        Passion flower blooms about this time. Apogee
        12.29hrs.

15th   Said to be fine day 6/7 years.

16th   Lunar eclipse.

18th   Perigee @ 1701hrs.

19th   A storm from the south indicates a mild winter may
        be expected.

20th – 22nd
        Barley set winds, 2/3 days of strong winds.

21st   St Mathew
        Brings the cold rain and dew, also 'shuts up the
        bees.'

22nd   Autumnal equinox @ 2202hrs = expect gales.
        September blow soft until fruits in loft. If weather
        warm today, the season should be fine, bright and
        clear this day, brings good wine in the next year. The
        day darkness overtakes light

29th   St Michael (Michaelmass).
        DoP. Quarter day. If it coincides with full moon
        will be a reliable guide for the next 45 days. An
        important quarter day for winds,

invariably giving the wind direction for the next
three months (to 21st December). Michaelmass
daisy flowers. So many days the old moon is – so
many floods after.

Met Office notes
1st to 17th Quiet period.

Buchan notes
none

General Notes and Comments

• The month of the patroness of Fruit trees and fruit – the
Goddess Pomona. The 'wood month' when wood was
gathered to lay-in for winter. The month of 'shedding' of
leaves, and fruit etc.

• The month of weather extremes.

• St Michaels Day -Quarter Day – Day of Prediction. If
it coincides with full moon will be reliable guide for the
next 45 days.

• [A fairly dependable indication as to the wind direction.
Beware however for this occurs around the period of
Equinoxes gales and may give a false reading locally. If
gales coincide with the Quarter Day wait for 2 days for
the wind to settle after the gales have subsided and then
get direction.]

- September is however a most unpredictable month and one should not be quick to jump to conclusions, as above.

- If St Michael brings many acorns, Christmas will cover the fields in snow.

- Foxgloves and Hollyhocks shed their leaves at the end of summer.

- As in September, so next March – and is often correct.

- Normally less rain than August. Average 80mm/3.5ins.

- If birds migrate early, indicates an early winter. If swallows fly off with summer, geese arrive with winter.

- If you crack open an Oak-apple on Michaelmass Day it reveals one of seven conditions. Each pattern predicts a different weather pattern for the year. These prophecies are accurate 9/10 years: 1. If spiders – there follows a naughty year. 2. If flies – A meetly good year. 3. If empty – a great dearth follows. 4. If lean – a hot dry summer. 5. If moist – a moist summer. 6. If kernel fair and clear – summer shall be fair and corn good too. 7. If many and ripen early – an early winter, and very much snow shall be before Christmas and that it shall be cold.

- Strong winds start this month and reach their peak on the 21st – about the time of the Equinox. These are called barleyset winds (barley harvest time).

- There are generally three consecutive windy days about the middle of the month. Windy barley harvest winds. Barleyset winds.

- 15th – Said to be fine 6/7 years. In fact, for any annual fixture dependant upon fine weather it would be difficult to choose a better date than the 15th.

- 20th, 21st and 22nd – These three days rule the weather for October, November and December.

- St Mathew (21st) brings the cold rain and dew, he also 'shut-up' the bees.

- When a cold spell occurs in September and passes off without a frost, a frost will not occur until the same time in October.

- Thunder in September indicates a good crop of fruit and grain for next year.

- When September has been rainy, the following May is generally dry, and when May is dry, September is apt to be wet. [check previous readings] The above is not really reliable – however – if May is well above the average for rain then the same can be said for September being above average for rain too.

and…

- If May is drier than average then September is likely to be drier than average too. All these from local personal figures.

- If acorns abound in September, snow will be deep in December. [true]

- If the storms in September clear off warm, all the storms the following winter will be warm.

- A fine Michaelmass sets all in tune. (fine weather until Martinmass (11th November).

- On Michaelmass the devil puts his foot on blackberries.

- If it does not rain on St Michael and Gallus (16th October), the following spring will be dry and propitious. (good omen).

- When summer meets winter it is a good augury for the coming spring.

- September dries up the ditches or breaks down bridges.

- If bunches of nuts do hang on branches after leaf-fall, it betokened a frosty winter with much snow. (true)

- During the second half of September, if a hard winter is due, the Robin will develop territory close to the house.

- London September average rainfall 49mms (1.3ins).

- Both droughts and floods are more likely to occur in September than August.

- Gallas is 16/10.

- A heavy apple crop points to a fine August and September.

- The month to celebrate the fruit of the wine.

The full moon this month is called HARVEST MOON

Tree of the month from 2nd to 29th is VINE. Thereafter the IVY.

Monthly averages for
Edenbridge (using 1981–2010 figures)

Mean Max:	20.8C
Mean Min:	9.2C
Mean Avg:	15C
Rainfall:	64.6mm
Sunshine:	185.8hrs

The following figures are for the average temperature at 12 noon and again at 4pm, taken at the beginning and again at the end of the month.

	12 noon	4pm
1st	20.37C	20.76C
30st	16.02C	16.71C

OCTOBER

NEW MOON = 1st @ 0113hrs = FROST AND
30th @1739hrs = FAIR

1ST QUARTER MOON = 9th @ 0535hrs = RAIN

FULL MOON 16th @ 0525hrs = RAIN

LAST QUARTER MOON 22nd @ 2016hrs = RAIN/SNOW

DOP = NONE THIS MONTH

HIGHEST SPRING TIDES 16th TO 21st

APOGEE 4th @ 1103hrs, AND 31st @ 1930hrs

PERIGEE 16th @ 2337hrs

DANGER WARNING: FULL MOON + PERIGEE + HIGHEST
SPRING TIDES

16th TO 21st EXPECT SEVERE WEATHER PROBLEMS

3rd   Day of celebration after wine harvest

4th   Apogee @ 1103hrs

11th   Vinalia Day
       New wine testing day. Apogee 14.18hrs

16th   Gallas
       see notes for 29th September. PERIGEE @ 2337hrs.

18th   St Luke
       St Luke's little summer is a fine day (4 days to a
       week of lovely weather)

25th   BST ENDS

28th   St Simon and St Jude Marks the end limit of St
       Luke's little summer. A rainy day. On St Jude's day
       the oxen may play (end of heavy farm work).

30th   BST ENDS

31st   Hallowtide
       If ducks swim at Hallowtide, at Christmas the same
       ducks will slide. The onset of winter and darker time
       of the year. Apogee @ 1930hrs

Met Office notes

16th to 19th Quiet period.

24th to 13th November a stormy period.

Buchan notes

None.

General Notes and Comments

- The Golden month – star of the weather prophets year.

- The month with more weather signs than any month, but it has no day of prediction.

- All October predictions look forward well into December and the New Year.

- October has 19/21 fine days, maybe over-optimistic, but usually more fine than rough.

- October forecast signs fit well with days of prediction, and should be taken seriously. Best reputation for long range forecasts.

- St Luke usually gives 4 days to a week of lovely weather. (very true) He does however sometimes arrive five days late!

- One can reasonably expect a warm period between mid-September and mid-November.

- Feast of St Simon and St Jude signals the start of a very stormy period, and the end of St Likes summer. It is also claimed there is never a year without rain this day.

- Abundance of acorns, dead nettles and thick onion skins in October indicate a hard winter.

- Heavy crop of haw-berries and beech nuts indicates a bad winter to come.

- 31st – Halloween. Has a reputation for being a quiet night.

- The garden month – expect downpours of rain.

- For every October fog there will be snow in winter, heavy or light according to the fog. Most reliable indeed.

- Full moon in October without frost, no frost till full moon in November. (a golden rule)

- If the October moon is born with the points up, the month will be dry. If down, wet. (the old saying being that a moon on its back catches the rain – a moon on its side cannot catch the rain)

- If during leaf-fall in October many leaves remain hanging, a frosty winter with much snow will follow. (very true)

- If in October leaves still hold, the coming winter will be cold (yes).

- Late leaf fall, hard in New Year, (true)

- If Oak bears its leaves in October there will be a hard winter. [very reliable]

- If in the fall of leaves many of them wither on the boughs and hang there, a frosty winter and much snow will follow. (proven yes)

- If foxes bark much in October they are calling up great falls of snow. (true even in Cities)

- (If no foxes or hares in your district watch the sheep. If they cluster together and move slowly, it is a sure sign of snow). Yes – proven with sheep.

- If the hare wears a thick coat in October, he shows his wisdom. (lay in a good stock of fuel)

- When owls hunt in daylight, expect a hard winter.

- If squirrels early mass their hoard, expect a winter like a sword.

- When birds and badgers are fat in October, you may expect a cold winter.

- If there is snow and frost in October, January will be mild.

- If October brings much frost and rain, then January and February will be mild.

- Windy October, dry January; warm October, cold February.

- If late October and early November are warm and rainy there is a better chance that January and February will be cold and frosty. (Proven from local records)

- October wet, March dry. [yes if October above average, March will be below average]

- October cold, March cold (is more likely from local records). October warm, March colder than average (proven from local records)

- The last week in October is the wettest of the year in southern England and the chances of a dry day on the 28th is minimal. [official averages]

- Observe the first heavy fog in August and expect a hard frost the same day in October. [check readings]

- Much rain in October, much wind/rain in December.

- When it freezes and snows in October, January will bring mild weather, but if it is thunder and lightning, the weather will resemble April in temper.

- If October brings heavy frosts and winds, then January and February will be mild.

- Redwings arrive mid-October and Fieldfares the end of October.

- In October dung your field and your land its wealth shall yield.

- The end of summer -leaves turn gold and fall, the chills of autumn herald the onset of winter.

- Wine harvest vintage month.

- Time of first frosts and final harvest. The greater the harvest, the greater the frost and snow the following winter.

The full moon this month is called the HUNTERS MOON.

The tree for the month is IVY up-to 27th. Thereafter it is the REED.

Monthly averages for
Edenbridge (using 1981–2010 figures)

Mean Max:	16C
Mean Min:	6.5C
Mean Avg:	11.25C
Rainfall:	92.9mm
Sunshine:	131.2hrs (day = 4.23hrs)

Whilst I appreciate the above are local figures, it will be an indication of what the averages are, and, of course there will be local variations. Such variations can be found by trawl-

ing the various weather websites, or by using the superb data found in the Climatologists Observers Link website.

The following figures are for the average temperature at 12 noon and again at 4pm, taken at the beginning and again at the end of the month.

	12 noon	4pm
1st	16C	17C
31st	11.8C	11.3C

The following figures are for the average temperature at 12 noon and again at 4pm, taken at the beginning and again at the end of the month.

	12 noon	4pm
1st	11.4C	10.8C
31st	8C	7.4C

NOVEMBER

NEW MOON = 29th @ 1219hrs = SNOW AND RAIN

1ST QUARTER MOON =7th @ 1952hrs = FAIR AND FROSTY

FULL MOON 14th @ 1353hrs = SNOW/RAIN + SUPERMOON

LAST QUARTER MOON 21st @ 0834hrs = COLD RAIN

DOP = 11th ST MARTIN

HIGHEST SPRING TIDES 14th TO 18th

APOGEE 27th @ 2009hrs: PERIGEE 14th @ 1124hrs

DANGER WARNING: FULL MOON + SUPERMOON + PERIGEE + HIGHEST SPRING TIDES

14th TO 18th EXPECT SEVERE WEATHER PROBLEMS

1st   All Saints

On November 1st if weather be clear, 'tis the end of sowing you'll do this year, weather will deteriorate thereafter with rain or frost.

2nd   All Souls Day

If wind SE it will stay until Candlemass (2/2) and winter will be mild with little snow.

10th   Martinmass Eve

Where the wind blows on Martinmass Eve, there 'twill be for the rest of winter.

11th   St Martin

DoP. The weather is said (reliably) to foretell the weather for three months (2/2) and so for the rest of winter. The onset of winter. Martlemass day.

14th   PERIGEE @ 1124hrs

21st   As this day so the winter.

23rd   St Clement

St Clement gives the winter – a fairly accurate quote.

25th   St Catherine

As St Catherine, foul or fair, so 'twill be next Februair. Laurel tree flowers about this time.

27th   Apogee @ 2009hrs Advent Sunday.

30th   St Andrew

Met Office notes

24th October to 13th stormy.

15th to 21st quiet.

24th to 14th December stormy.

Buchan notes

6th to 13th cold period.

General Notes and Comments.

- The Black month. Drab foggy depressing weather.

- The month when the sun loses its power. The first month of the winter quarter.

- The weather St Martins Day (11th) will fortell the weather for 3 months AND where the wind blows on the 10th it will remain for the winter. REINFORCED by wind at NW on Martinmass and severe winter to come.

- The above sayings and observations need heeding for they often add up to a very very accurate picture.

- Any time around St Martins Day expect a short spell of fine weather 'St Martins Summer', lasting three days and a bit.

- 11th – Leaves on trees and grape vines this day indicate a hard winter (proven). WNW wind this day indicates a severe winter (proven). If a SW wind this day it will remain until old Candlemass (2/2) with a mild winter up to then and no snow to speak of.

- If dry fair and cold on Martinmass, the cold in winter will not last long.

- If All Saints Day (1st) brings out winter then St Martins will bring Indian summer. If a beech nut be found dry, a hard winter – If wet and not light, expect a wet winter.

- Flowers in bloom indicate a hard winter.

- St Clements (23rd) is the first day of winter, and is said to give the weather for February.
- If new moon on 13th and full moon on the 28th – look for a change in the weather.
- Expect both rain and frost after the 1st.
- If ice in November will bear a duck, then the rest of winter is slush and muck.
- If late October and early November be warm and rainy, then January and February shall be frosty and cold.
- If leaves not fall by Martinmass then a cruel winter's on its way.
- Sybil of months and worshipper of winds I love thee, rude and boisterous as thou art.
- November cold, Christmas warm. – wistful
- Ice in November brings slush in December.
- If the water freezes in November, January will be all the wetter.
- No warmth, no cheerfulness, no healthful ease, no comfortable feeling in any member,
- No shade, no sun, no butterflies, no bees, no fruit, no flowers, no leaves, November.
- When in November the water (table) rises, it will show itself the whole winter.
- A miserable month.
- Thunder in November, a fertile year to come.

The name of the full moon this month is FOG MOON.

The tree of the month up-to 24th is the REED. Thereafter the ELDER.

Monthly averages for
Edenbridge (using 1981–2010 figures)

Mean Max: 11.1C
Mean Min: 3.4C
Mean Avg: 7.25C
Rainfall: 85.1mm
Sunshine: 87.8hrs (day = 2.93hrs)

	12 noon	4pm
1st	11.4C	10.8C
30th	8C	7.4C

DECEMBER

NEW MOON = 29th @ 0654hrs = STORMY

1ST QUARTER MOON = 7th @ 0930hrs = COLD RAIN

FULL MOON = 14th @ 0006hrs = FROST

LAST QUARTER MOON 21st @ 0156hrs = FROST

DOP = 21st ST THOMAS'S

SOLSTICE 21st @ 1044hrs

HIGHEST SPRING TIDES 13th TO 18th

APOGEE 25th @ 0556hrs: PERIGEE 12th @ 2328hrs

DANGER WARNING: FULL MOON + PERIGEE + HIGHEST SPRING TIDES

13th TO 18th EXPECT SEVERE WEATHER PROBLEMS

4th	2nd in Advent
5th	Apogee 14.57hrs
6th	St Nicolas
	2nd Sunday in Advent
11th	3rd in Advent
12th	Apogee 2304hrs
	Perigee @ 2328hrs
18th	4th Sunday in Advent
21st	St Thomas
	DoP. Quarter Day, Shortest day of the year Winter Solstice. Weather up to 2/2.
25th	Christmas Day Holly and Ivy flower about this time. Apogee @0556hrs.
26th	St Stephen
	Boxing Day
27th	St John
28th	Childermass/Innocents Day
	Unluckiest day of the year when no work should be started. See notes below.
31st	Hogmanay
	Celebrates the solar divinity of Hogmanay.

Met Office notes

Stormy carried forward from 24th November to 14th.
Quiet period 15th to 21st.
Stormy 25th to 31st.

Buchan notes

3rd to 14th warm period.

General Notes and Comments

- Expect gale force winds. The portents generally threaten a nasty month, but a hint of better things to come with the worst over. It ought however to be over by the end of January.

- 21st – 31st normally/traditionally a stormy period.

- Day of Prediction (21st) portends weather until 2nd February and the direction of the prevailing wind up to the vernal equinox on 21st March. If it freezes this day the price of corn will fall – which implies a good harvest – but also a hard winter.

- If however mild, the price of corn will rise.

- If Christmas falls on a Sunday, it shall be a warm winter, the summer hot and dry.

- If Christmas day and Thursday be – a windy winter will shall see.

- If it rains on the first Sunday of December, before mass, it will rain for a week.

- Christmas can be Green – in the old sense of 'bright' (clear/light and bright) – yielding a good harvest (proven) – a peaceful year of plenty.

- Black – will bode ill for next year's weather. White – a muddy Easter. Warm – a cold Easter. Wet – empty granary and barrel. Windy – trees will bring much fruit, but if the weather grows stormy before sunset, it betokened sickness in the spring and summer quarters. Snow – good hay crop next year.

- But if the Milky Way shows clear you may safely count on a fruitful year. [This can be a good indicator]

- If it snows during Christmas night, the crops will do well.

- Light Christmas, light wheat sheaf – dark Christmas, heavy wheat sheaf (if full moon about Christmas Day)

- If Christmas ice hangs on the willow, clover may be cut at Easter.

- A windy Christmas and a calm Candlemass are signs of a good year.

- Thunder in December presages fine weather.

- Thunder during Christmas week indicates that there will be much snow during the winter.

- A Green Christmas means a full churchyard.

- If Christmas Day be on a Saturday, the weather be great with wind, snow and cold, the summer good and there shall be war in many lands. (except the last, quite accurate)

- If berries on trees at Christmas, they'll stay 'til snow is down. If gone then a mild winter.

- St Thomas Day is always grey. the longest night and the shortest day.

- A dull Christmas with no sun, bodes ill for the harvest.

- When the sun shines through the apple trees on Christmas Day, when Autumn comes, they will a load of fruit display. [reliable – also indicates a good Spring with few late frosts, frost-free May and a good Autumn.]

- If ice bears before Christmas, it won't bear a goose afterwards.

- Christmas in snow, Easter in mud. Easter in snow, Christmas in mud.

- If much rain during the 12 days of Christmas a wet year to come.

- If on a New Years Eve the winds blow south, it betokened warmth and growth.

- If west, much milk and fish in the sea. If north, cold and storms there will be.

- If east, the trees will bear much fruit. If north-east, then flee it man and beast.

- 26th – If windy, bad for next years grapes.

- 28th Childermass Day – if lowering and wet there will be scarcity. If fair it promises plenty.

- Much rain in October. much wind in December. [check October readings]

- In December, keep yourself warm, and sleep.

- A winter fog will freeze a dog.

- Every mile is two in winter.

- 25/12 to 5/1. These 12 days are said to be the keys of the weather for the whole year.

The full moon this month is called THE HUNTING/COLD MOON.

The tree up-to the 22nd is the ELDER. There is no tree on the 23rd. The BIRCH then becomes the monthly tree.

Monthly averages for
Edenbridge (using 1981–2010 figures)

Mean Max:	8.1C
Mean Min:	1.9C
Mean Avg:	5C
Rainfall:	85.8mm
Sunshine:	64.6hrs (day = 2.08hrs)

The following figures are for the average temperature at 12 noon and again at 4pm, taken at the beginning and again at the end of the month.

	12 noon	4pm
1st	8.2C	7.3C
31st	5.5C	5C

Some Suggestions for Reading

Natural Weather Wisdom (Uncle Offa)
ISBN 1 85421 151X

Weatherlore (Richard Inwards)
ISBN 0946014 77 9

Forecasting the Country Way (Robin Page)
Penguin books

Red Sky at Night (Ian Currie)
ISBN 0951670 2 2

Weatherwise (Alan Watts)
ISBN 978 0 7136 8153 6

The Weather of Britain (Robin Sterling)
ISBN 1900357 06

Weatherwise (Philip Eden)
ISBN 0 333 6160 3

Synoptic Climatology (Berry and Perry)
ISBN 416 085008 8

The Met Office book of British Weather
ISBN 978 0 7153 3640 3

The Climate of the British Isles (Chandler and Gregory)
ISBN 0 582 48558

Climate of the Modern World (Lamb)
ISBN 0416 334407

Elementary Meteorology (Met Office)
ISBN 0 11 400312 2

The Weather Handbook (Watts)
ISBN 1 84037 0890

The Daily Telegraph Great British Weather (Eden)
ISBN 978 0 8264 72610

The Daily Telegraph Book of the Weather (Eden)
ISBN 0 8264 61972

Marine Observers Handbook (Met Office)
ISBN ISBN 0 11 400367X

Observers Handbook (Met Office)
ISBN 0 400329 7

Yesterday's Weather (Roy Bradford)
ISBN 978 1 905546 42 8

Weather Observers Handbook (Burt)
ISBN 978 1 107 66228 5

Daily Telegraph Change the Weather (Eden)
ISBN 0 8264 8029 2

Collins Weather – the ultimate guide to the elements
ISBN 10 0002200643

Oxford Weather Facts (File)
ISBN 0 19 2861433

Oxford Dictionary of Weather (Dunlop)
ISBN 0 19 2800639

Teach Yourself Weather (Hardy)
ISBN 0 340 62707 7

Collins Complete Guide to British Insects
ISBN 10 000 7298994

Collins Complete Guide to Wild Flowers
ISBN 10 000 7236840

Collins Complete Guide to British Trees
ISBN 10 000 7211775

RSPB Pocket Guide to British Birds
ISBN 10 140 8174561

A Private Life of an English Field (Lewis-Stemper)
ISBN 978 0 552 77899 2

The Running Hare (Lewis-Stemper)
ISBN 978 0 857 523266

I have compiled much of this book using extracts from most, if not all, of the above books, plus extracts from various websites.

A fuller list of the website sources can be found at http://www.weatherwithouttechnology.co.uk

The Beaufort Wind Scale

The Beaufort Scale was invented by Admiral Sir Francis Beaufort (1774–1857) in 1805 to help sailors describe the wind conditions at sea. It has since been adapted for use on land. By using this chart a person can gauge wind speed. The use of instruments that can accurately measure wind speed has superseded the scale, however it is still in popular use.

The Beaufort Wind Scale (Water)

Beaufort Number	Description	Knots	Sea Condition
0	Calm	0	Sea like a mirror
1	Light Air	1–3	Ripples but no foam crests
2	Light Breeze	4–6	Small wavelets, crests do not break
3	Gentle Breeze	7–10	Large wavelets, scattered white horses
4	Moderate Breeze	11–16	Small waves, frequent white horses
5	Fresh Breeze	17–21	Moderate waves, many white horses
6	Strong Breeze	22–27	Large waves forming, white foam crests
7	Near Gale	28-33	Sea heaps up and white foam blown in streaks
8	Gale	34–40	Moderately high waves, crests break into spindrift
9	Severe Gale	41–47	High waves crests begin to roll over, dense foam, lots of spray
10	Storm	48–55	Very high waves with overhanging crests. Sea becomes white
11	Violent Storm	56–63	Exceptionally high waves, sea covered with long patches of foam
12	Hurricane	64+	Air filled with foam and spray. Sea white with driving spray

The Beaufort Wind Scale (Land)

Beaufort Number	Description	Km/h	Visual
0	Calm	0–2	Smoke rises vertically
1	Light Air	2–5	Smoke drifts slowly
2	Slight Breeze	6–12	Leaves rustle
3	Gentle Breeze	13–20	Leaves and twigs in motion
4	Moderate Breeze	21–29	Small branches move
5	Fresh Breeze	30–39	Small trees sway
6	Strong Breeze	40–50	Large branches sway
7	Moderate Gale	51–61	Whole trees in motion
8	Fresh Gale	62–74	Twigs break off trees
9	Strong Gale	75–87	Branches break
10	Whole Gale	88–101	Trees snap and are blown down
11	Storm	102–115	Widespread damage
12	Hurricane	116–130	Extreme damage

Weather notes

Weather notes